Make Your Own

UKULELE

Make Your Own
UKULELE

THE ESSENTIAL GUIDE TO BUILDING, TUNING, AND LEARNING TO PLAY THE UKE

BILL PLANT

Fox Chapel
PUBLISHING

ABOUT THE AUTHOR

Bill Plant was raised in rural Australia, where he spent a lot of time tinkering in his dad's workshop. This hobby allowed Plant to gain skills making objects out of wood and creating stained glass. Plant studied visual and performing arts at Charles Sturt University and later studied joinery at the Goulburn Ovens Institute of Technical and Further Education, where he eventually became an instructor in joinery, furniture making, and furniture design. Plant has been making instruments for ten years and ukuleles for about five. He still lives in rural Australia, where he plays music, writes a bit, and continues creating instruments.

Author Bill Plant at home.

Many thanks to Paul Celentano, Luke R. Davies, Jerry Hoffman, Peter Hurney, Jay Lichty and Corrie Woods of Lichty Guitars, Daniel Luiggi, Char and Gordon Mayer and Aaron Keim of Mya-Moe Ukuleles, Chuck Moore, John and Pam Ramsey or Palm Tree Ukuleles, Keith Ogata, and Gary Zimnicki for submitting photos of their work for the ukulele gallery.

The photo of Bill Tapia on page 76 has been used under the Creative Commons Attribution 2.0 Generic (CC BY 2.0) license. For more information, visit *http://creativecommons.org/licenses*.

ISBN 978-1-56523-565-6

Library of Congress Cataloging-in-Publication Data

Plant, Bill.
 Make your own ukulele / Bill Plant.
   p. cm.
 Includes index.
 ISBN 978-1-56523-565-6
 1. Ukulele--Construction. I. Title.
 ML1015.U5P53 2012
 787.8'91923--dc23
                    2011031479

To learn more about the other great books from Fox Chapel Publishing, or to find a retailer near you, call toll-free 800-457-9112 or visit us at *www.FoxChapelPublishing.com*.

Note to Authors: We are always looking for talented authors to write new books in our area of woodworking, design, and related crafts. Please send a brief letter describing your idea to Acquisition Editor, 1970 Broad Street, East Petersburg, PA 17520.

Printed in China
First printing

About This Book

A good ukulele with an easy action and beautiful tone is a delight to play, but a ukulele with those qualities is usually very expensive unless you make your own. That may sound like a daunting task, but making your own ukulele is easy if you follow the steps in this book.

This book tells you all you need to know to make two different ukuleles. The "boxer" has a rectangular body and can be built from scratch or a cigar box. Either way, you don't need special woodworking skills or fancy equipment—just basic hand tools.

If you're more adept or feeling more adventurous, try the professional-grade, solid-wood ukulele project. You can make it in a home workshop using basic woodworking equipment and a minimum of specialist luthier tools. You can design your own ukulele (the gallery of custom-made ukuleles from around the world on pages 12–31 and our design advice will whet your appetite), or you can use the plans in Chapter 4.

The construction process is broken down into a logical series of steps, with photographs and drawings to make everything clear and easy to follow. Throughout, you'll find some tricks of the trade and handy hints on how to fix the mistakes that everyone makes from time to time.

One way to keep the mistakes to a minimum is practice: Try each step on scrap wood until you are comfortable with the process and then proceed to build your ukulele with confidence. When I first decided to make my own ukulele, I thought I would make two at once in case I messed one up. To get myself started, I broke the construction process down into simple steps. Whenever I encountered a new step, I took a piece of scrap wood and practiced until I gained enough confidence in my work to comfortably proceed with the project uke. Guess what? They both turned out fine.

Using this book, you will also learn how to tune your ukulele's soundboard to create an instrument with its own unique sound. You'll learn how to set up the action for fast, clean playing, and how to give your new ukulele the finish it deserves.

I have been playing one of my early ukes for a number of years. It has a patch of light fingernail dents in the soundboard, the fingerboard has indentations worn in from playing chords, the lacquer is starting to wear through in some places, and there are a few other dings here and there. In other places it has developed a beautiful patina from being handled and played. Over the years, it has acquired a lovely rich tone and is an absolute delight to play. I know it will continue to improve with playing, and that is the best part of all.

—BILL PLANT

Contents

An Introduction to the Ukulele

Before you begin the process of building your own ukulele, you might want to understand its history or learn about its musical qualities. Here is some information that you might find useful as you begin the process of building and playing your own ukulele.

Ukulele Fact:
The ukulele was once known as the taro patch fiddle in Hawaii.

A BRIEF HISTORY

In the 1870s, many Portuguese immigrants arrived in Hawaii to work in the sugarcane fields, bringing along a traditional Portuguese instrument, the *machete*. It was not long before native interest grew in this new arrival and Hawaiians began making their own version of the instrument. They based their design on the small guitar-like *machete* and called it a ukulele. The Hawaiians found their local woods, notably koa, made brilliant-sounding instruments.

The ukulele became a very popular jazz instrument throughout North America during the 1920s. Inexpensive and easy to play, it was also a widely used parlor instrument. In fact, you can find ukulele chord charts on the popular sheet music of the time. The rise of rock and roll in the 1950s, fueled by the guitar, sent the ukulele into obscurity. The instrument experienced a revival in the 1990s, however, which has since snowballed into a mass movement.

Now, ukuleles are everywhere. People have once again discovered the ukulele is an easy instrument to play, yet so versatile it can make almost any style of music or song sound great. Experienced musicians see another side to the ukulele: complex chord patterns and rhythms that take this simple instrument to another level.

What's in a Name?

It is unclear how the ukulele got its present name, but several theories seem plausible. Translated, ukulele means "jumping flea," which many feel reflects the musician's quick finger movement over the instrument.

Ukulele was the nickname of Edward Purvis, Hawaiian King Kalakaua's chamberlain. Purvis was also a talented *machete* player, and the instrument might have inherited his name. Ukulele also translates as "the gift that came from afar," so the instrument's name might refer to its Portuguese origins. Finally, it's possible that ukulele is the shortened version of *ukeke-lele*, or dancing *ukeke*. The *ukeke* is a Hawaiian stringed instrument similar to the ukulele.

UKULELE ANATOMY

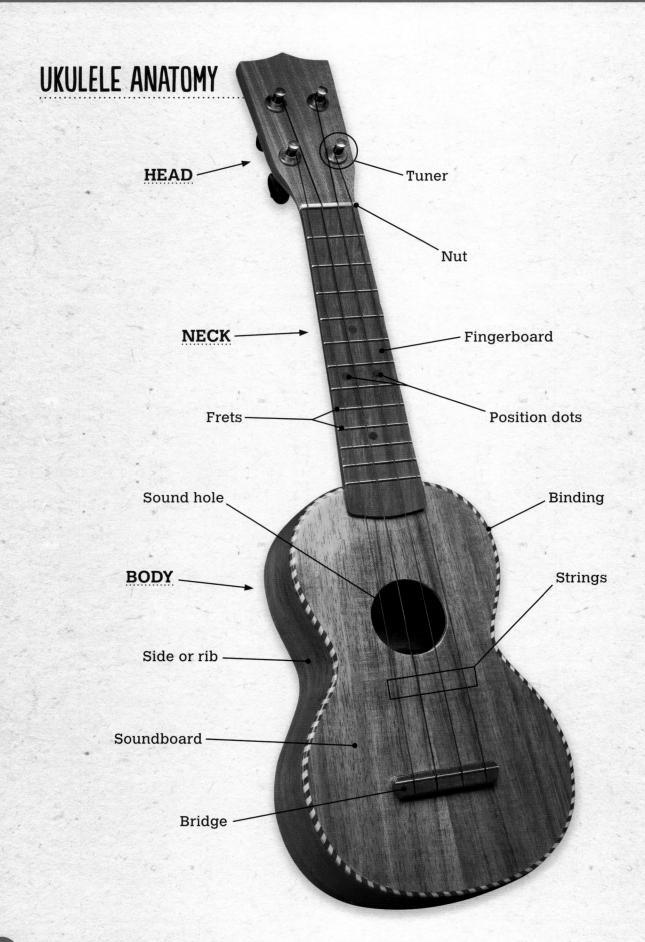

HEAD

Tuner

Nut

NECK

Fingerboard

Frets

Position dots

Sound hole

Binding

BODY

Strings

Side or rib

Soundboard

Bridge

TYPES OF UKULELES

Soprano

Concert

Tenor

Baritone

Soprano. The soprano ukulele is a bright-sounding instrument. It is the smallest ukulele, about 21" (533mm) long overall, and has always been the most popular ukulele size by far. The scale length (the distance between the nut and the bridge) is usually about 13" (330mm).

Concert. Slightly larger than the soprano, the concert ukulele has a deeper sound and a little more volume than its smaller counterpart. It is about 23" (584mm) long, with a scale length of about 15" (381mm). The vocal range of a concert ukulele makes it a nice complement to the higher-pitched soprano. Some concert ukulele players replace the fourth, or top G, string with a low G string, which deepens the instrument's tonal range.

Tenor. Deeper and louder than a concert ukulele, the tenor ukulele is sometimes fitted with a spruce soundboard that can increase its volume. Some tenor ukuleles can sound a little harsh and need to be played quietly in a group session to keep from drowning out the other instruments. A tenor ukulele is about 26" (660mm) long, with a scale length of about 17" (432mm).

Baritone. This large ukulele has a deep tone and different tuning from the others. A baritone ukulele's strings are tuned to the notes D, G, B, and E, which correspond to the first four strings of a guitar. The chords for this ukulele are therefore really abbreviated guitar chords, which makes it easier for a guitar player to progress to playing a ukulele. A baritone ukulele is about 30" (762mm) long, with a scale length of about 19" (483mm). A "bass" ukulele is just a baritone ukulele body fitted with a wide neck that has a 20" (508mm) scale length, polyurethane bass strings, and an under-saddle piezo pickup. It is tuned in the same manner as a bass guitar. A bass ukulele is very soft on its own, but sounds great when played through an amplifier. It has a warm sound, almost like that of a double bass, which makes it very popular with ukulele groups.

A UKULELE GALLERY

So you think you know what a ukulele looks like? These examples from ukulele producers around the world demonstrate the wide range of ukulele design possibilities. When you go to design your own instrument, don't hesitate to think outside the box.

Paul Celentano, North Carolina

Paul Celentano brings a light-hearted creativity to ukulele creation. Celentano has always held an interest in musical instruments and the physics behind them. Seeking to combine his love of art, music, and woodworking, Celentano started Celentano Woodworks in 2008 and established a presence on Etsy. Celentano strives to combine style with functionality, something he's done since he designed his first stringed instrument in the shape of a lizard at age fifteen. Using this type of creativity, Celentano now designs and creates one-of-a-kind instruments, custom tailored to the instrumentalist's personal tastes, like a favorite food, animal, or object. Celentano's designs are also *fun*: fun to make, fun to look at, and fun to play. See more at *http://www.etsy.com/shop/celentanowoodworks*.

Below Left: Cupcake Ukulele. Tenor ukulele, body size 9" x 10" x 2" (229 x 254 x 51mm). Made from maple, poplar, and basswood. Hand painted and finished with acrylics.

Below Middle: Heart Ukulele. Baritone/tenor ukulele, body size 11" x 12" x 2½" (279 x 305 x 64mm). Made from maple, poplar, and basswood. Red lacquer finish.

Below Right: Blue Burst Les Paul Ukulele. Tenor ukulele, body size 9" x 11" x 2½" (229 x 279 x 64mm). Made from maple and ipê. Blue burst lacquer finish.

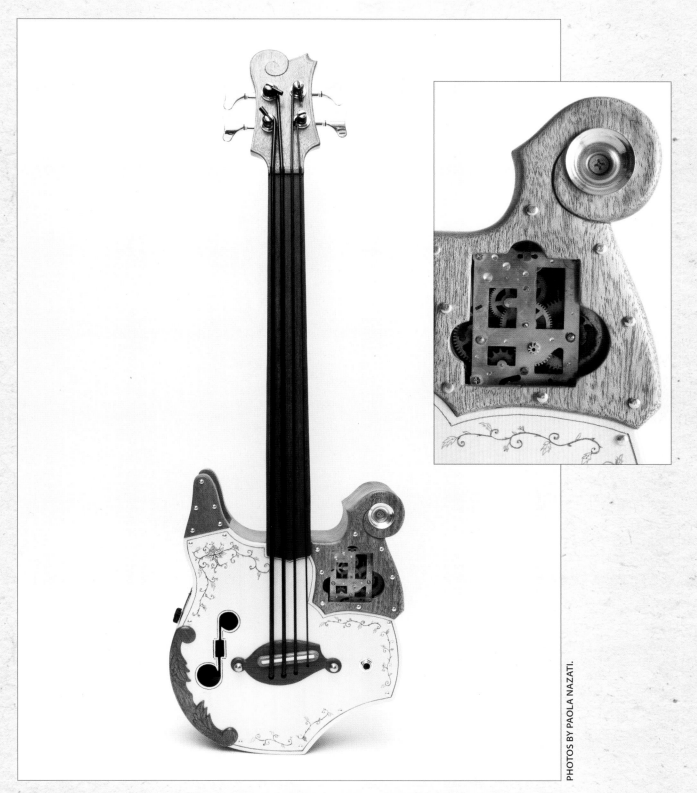

PAUL CELENTANO

Steampunk Ukulele Bass. Body size 10" x 12" x 3¼" (254 x 305 x 83mm). Made from maple, sepal, mahogany, ipê, spruce, and brass and steel findings, such as clock parts, gears, nails, horns, wire, and other found materials. Hand-drawn pen and ink detailing.

Luke R. Davies, Australia

Luke has been a professional musician for more than twenty years and builds instruments from cigar boxes, old hubcaps, and other found objects. Luke's instruments may look quirky, but they sound sensational and he plays them professionally. See more at *www.lukerdavies.com*.

The soprano cigar-box ukulele (left) has an Australian hardwood neck and an inexpensive piezo pickup attached to the soundboard. Davies spent a great deal of time experimenting with the placement of the pickup to produce the optimum sound quality. The concert banjo ukulele (right) makes use of a bongo drum for the soundboard, a traditional floating bridge, and a hubcap resonator. The hardwood neck runs through the body of the ukulele like a traditional banjo.

Jerry Hoffmann, Missouri

Jerry Hoffmann's ukuleles show some unique design and construction methods. He specializes in original design and handcrafted construction. Learn more at *www.boatpaddleukuleles.com.*

M-style concert ukulele made by Boat Paddle Ukulele Co. This ukulele differs from traditional concert ukuleles with a lower body that is wider than usual—giving the instrument more bass presence—a horizontal neck joint, four-element fan bracing, and a pinned nut.

Peter Hurney, California

Peter Hurney was born to a good Boston home and gained many artistic skills in his early life. Hurney eventually moved to Hawaii, where, in his words, he "learned to make a pretty good ukulele." It wasn't long before his instrument-making skills rose to match the level of his artistic skills.

Hurney now lives in Berkeley, California, where he runs his instrument-making shop, Pohaku Instruments. At Pohaku, Hurney designs and builds great-sounding and fanciful instruments, fulfilling the desires of ukulele enthusiasts from all over the world. Hurney's ukuleles range from traditional designs, to elegant art deco-style instruments, to whimsical compositions reflecting the character and interests of each owner. Learn more at *www.pohakuukulele.com*.

Below Left: *Kitten's Uke,* **2008.** Concert ukulele made of western cedar, Honduran mahogany, ebony, mother-of-pearl, and silk-screened piano keys with a lacquer finish. This instrument was built for San Francisco-based performer Miss Kitten on the Keys.

Below Right: *Seafoam,* **2009.** Concert ukulele made of Sitka spruce, Claro walnut, and a plastic toilet seat with tinted lacquer.

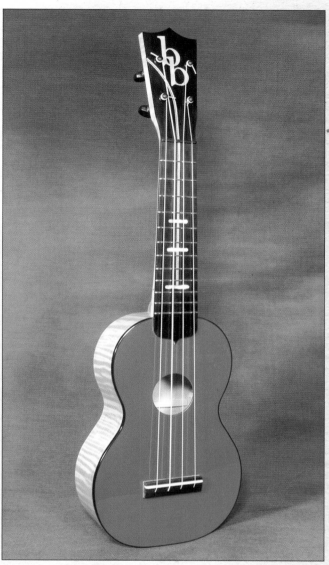

Bliss Blood, 2008. Built for Brooklyn-based performer Bliss Blood, this soprano ukulele is made of western curly maple, Sitka spruce, and ebony with mother-of-pearl inlay and tinted lacquer.

Cubist, 2006. This Picasso-inspired concert ukulele is made of koa, spruce, and ebony with tinted lacquer.

Jay Lichty, North Carolina

Award-winning luthier Jay Lichty built his first ukulele for fun and found there was no looking back. Under the guidance of master luthier Wayne Henderson, Lichty quickly mastered the skills of guitar building. Today, Lichty focuses on developing instruments with perfect tone, striving for each one's voice to be to the ukulele what a Stradivarius is to the violin. No two Lichty ukuleles are alike, a feat made possible by Lichty's close collaboration with each and every one of his customers during the instrument's creation, making the process interactive from start to finish. While Lichty's instruments are heirloom-quality works of art, they are also fun to play, fun to listen to, and have the wonderful ability to fuel creative expression. See more at *http://lichtyguitars.com*.

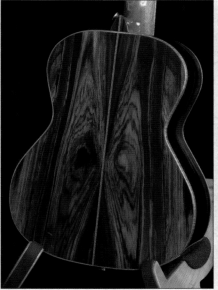

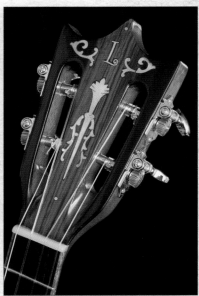

Brazillian Rosewood Tenor Ukulele with Red Cedar Top, 26¼" (667mm) long, 5⅞" (149mm) wide at the waist. Brazillian rosewood back, sides, and headplate; ebony bridge and fretboard; red cedar top; koa binding; bone nut and saddle; Grover tuners; pearl inlay; K&K Sound pickup. Jay Lichty created this ukulele for himself and plays it at his music performances.

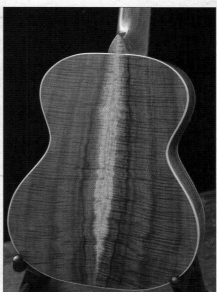

JAY LICHTY

Hand Painted Koa Tenor Ukulele, 26¼" (667mm) long, 5⅞" (149mm) wide at the waist. Koa back, sides, and headplate; Engelmann spruce top; maple binding and rosette; ebony fretboard and bridge; bone nut and saddle; Grover tuners. This ukulele is one of four instruments representing a collaboration between luthier Jay Lichty and artist Clark Hipolito. All four instruments were part of the "Birds of a Feather" art exhibition in Wilmington, North Carolina.

PHOTOS BY CORRIE WOODS OF LICHTY GUITARS.

Pau Ferro Tenor Ukulele, 26¼" (667mm) long, 5⅞" (149mm) wide at the waist. Pau ferro back, sides, and headplate; sinker redwood top; paua abalone rosette; ebony fretboard and bridge; bone nut and saddle; cocobolo binding; Gotoh tuners. The customer for whom this ukulele was designed hand selected each piece of wood and component for the instrument. The sinker redwood used for the top refers to wood from redwood logs felled in California during the late 1800s. The logs were buried under riverbeds during the logging process and were later salvaged.

Brazilian Rosewood Tenor Ukulele with Sinker Redwood Top, 26¼" (667mm) long, 5⅞" (149mm) wide at the waist. Brazilian rosewood back, sides, and headplate; sinker redwood top; koa with mother of pearl binding/purfling; ebony fretboard and bridge; bone nut and saddle; mother-of-pearl rosette; Grover tuners. Custom designed and built for a renowned California magician, this ukulele is lovingly called the Magic Ukulele.

Brazilian Rosewood Tenor Ukulele with Curly Redwood Top, 26¼" (667mm) long, 5⅞" (149mm) wide at the waist. Brazilian Rosewood back, sides, and headplate; curly redwood top; ebony fretboard and bridge; bone nut and saddle; koa binding; maple rosette; Gotoh tuners. Lichty custom designed and built this ukulele for Julie Strietelmeier, owner and operator of *http://ukulelereview.com.*

Koa Tenor Ukulele, 26¼" (667mm) long, 5⅞" (149mm) wide at the waist. Koa back, sides, and top; ebony fretboard and bridge; mahogany neck; mother-of-pearl inlay and rosette; curly maple binding; Grover tuners. A family commissioned this ukulele as a gift for a loved one, celebrating his achievements.

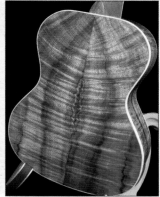

PHOTOS BY CORRIE WOODS OF LICHTY GUITARS.

Created in 2011, this tenor ukulele features an alerce top; Indian rosewood back and sides; cedro neck; Brazilian rosewood bridge; and an ebony binding, nut, saddle, and fretboard. The instrument was finished with a French polish applied by hand.

Constructed using materials from places like Canada, Brazil, Argentina, and India, this ukulele features a red cedar top; cedro back and sides; a lenga neck; palo santo fretboard and bridge; urunday head; and an ebony saddle and nut.

Daniel Luiggi, Argentina

Daniel Luiggi, a luthier from Buenos Aires, has a keen interest in the technological and acoustic aspects of instrument design. As a musician, Luiggi has fully committed himself to the production of high-quality musical instruments, specializing in concert guitars, ukuleles, and the Venezuelan cuatro. Until 2006, he was an active member of the DAMA Lutheria group, an organization that received a grant from the State Secretary of Culture (Argentina), allowing Luiggi to research wood engineering and apply his findings to the building of stringed instruments using Argentine woods. After leaving the group, Luiggi has continued this research on his own. See more at *www.luiggiluthier.com*.

Chuck Moore, Hawaii

Chuck Moore builds custom ukuleles from locally grown koa trees in his solar-powered shop on the Big Island of Hawaii. The sound holes he crafts are often anything but round, and he embellishes his instruments with intriguing inlays. See more at *www.moorebettahukes.com*.

Super-Soprano Pineapple. Made of maple-bound koa, this unique ukulele has a soprano-scale body with a concert-scale neck and custom rope purfling.

Howzit Brah? Moore built this tenor ukulele using koa for every component.

Cutaway tenor ukulele. Blonde koa with bamboo, gold mother-of-pearl, and bloodwood inlay.

Mother-of-pearl inlay gives extra shine to the wave detail around this ukulele's sound hole.

Mya-Moe Ukuleles, Washington

Mya-Moe Ukuleles is a team composed of Char and Gordon Mayer, husband and wife, and their good friend and luthier Aaron Keim. This trio hand-builds about 250 ukuleles each year, focusing on bringing professional-quality acoustics and playability to what has traditionally been a "campfire" instrument. Often described as having "punch" or "sparkle," Mya-Moe instruments are known for their beautiful voices.

The company offers instruments with a playability feature set, which includes perfect intonation, a radiused fretboard, and a hand-shaped neck with inlaid graphite. These invaluable features are largely responsible for the ninety-plus professional touring musicians who play Mya-Moe instruments, including Dave Matthews, Ben Harper, Eddie Vedder, Jerry Douglas, and Marcus Mumford. See more at *www.myamoeukuleles.com*.

PHOTOS BY GORDON MAYER.

#500 Master-Grade Myrtle Tenor Cutaway Classic, 2011, 26" (660mm) long and 5¾" (146mm) wide at the waist. This Classic-style ukulele is one of Mya-Moe's best sellers. This model, made of walnut, myrtle, and ebony, includes a cutaway feature and abalone inlays.

#585 Red Maple Super Soprano Classic, 2011, 22" (559mm) long and 4³⁄₁₆" (106mm) wide at the waist. Bloodwood binding adds a unique touch to this Classic-style ukulele, which has a soprano-sized body and a concert-sized scale length (neck).

Make Your Own Ukulele An Introduction to the Ukulele

Keith Ogata, Hawaii

Unlike many artisans, Keith Ogata, owner of ASD Hawaii Ukuleles, is guided by the concept that form must follow function. When creating a ukulele, his first goal is to create an instrument that produces great sound qualities (for without great sound it ends up being just a beautiful box). That is the function. Once the function has been established, a style, the form, can wrap itself around that great sound. Ogata's first ukulele, the *Kinohi*, perfectly follows this concept. The bends and angles of the instrument are purposefully placed to direct sound waves in an attempt to lengthen and therefore deepen the resulting tone.

Ogata recognizes listening is a necessary component of building a ukulele, knowing he can get the wood to ring by persuading it in the proper fashion. He believes there are no boundaries to design, including ukulele design, saying, "We have not even made the large strides required to change the ukulele to what it can eventually become, of which, changing perception might be the greatest challenge." See more at *www.asdhawaii.com*.

Above Left: *Kinohi.* Koa body and bridge; maple binding; maple and koa neck; ebony saddle, fingerboard, and nut; and Grover tuners. Meaning "beginning" in Hawaiian, the *Kinohi* was Ogata's first ukulele design.

Above Middle: *Oko'a.* Koa body, bridge, neck, and fingerboard; maple binding; ebony saddle and nut; and compression tuners. Oko'a, meaning "different" combines the concepts of producing low notes with a large instrument body and producing high notes with a small instrument body.

Above Right: *PD-3.* Sapele body and neck; koa soundboard and fingerboard; maple binding and saddle; walnut bridge; ebony nut; and Grover tuners. The *PD-3* mimics the design of a guitar, giving the ukulele a bluesy sound.

Palm Tree Ukuleles, Colorado

John and Pam Ramsey make ukuleles based on classic styles from 1920 to 1949, using a variety of bindings, rosettes, and inlays. John, a longtime maker of guitars and mandolins, added ukuleles to his repertoire in 2005. The ukuleles are made from koa, selected for its beauty and tonal qualities. Learn more at *http://palmtreeukuleles.com*.

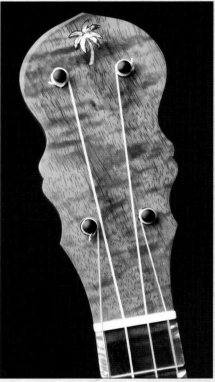

The concert ukulele in these photos is made of highly figured koa wood in the vintage Hawaiian style, with ebony peghead tuners. The binding and inlay on the fingerboard is mother-of-pearl.

Bill Plant, Australia

The author uses Australian hardwoods to chase tone and beauty. This soprano ukulele is made from Australian blackwood. The author enjoys working with this wood because of its tone and striking features.

Concert ukulele. Figured Queensland maple with river red gum fingerboard and binding.

Gary Zimnicki, Michigan

Flexibility in instrument design and construction enables Gary Zimnicki to match each customer's individual requirements. Here, you can see how careful book-matching of the wood enhances both the front and back of the instrument. See more at *www.zimnicki.com*.

This concert ukulele measures 7⅞" (200mm) across the lower body and has a scale length of 15¼" (387mm). It has a koa body, ebony fretboard, peghead veneer, rosewood bridge, and friction peg tuners and is finished with high-gloss nitrocellulose lacquer. A notable feature is the three-piece mahogany and maple neck, with a Spanish heel neck and body joint.

CHAPTER 1

Designing Your Ukulele

The body of a ukulele is a hollow box that amplifies the sound of the vibration of plucked strings and broadcasts it through a hole on the front of the instrument.

Ukulele Fact:
Samuel Kamaka made the first pineapple ukulele in the 1920s.

The body has curved sides, with internal wood blocks supporting each end of the side pieces. The top and bottom are glued to the sides at a joint strengthened by a thin strip of wood called lining. The neck is attached to the body by a mortise, or butt, joint at the end block. The neck itself is simply a shaped piece of solid wood that holds the fingerboard, nut, and tuners.

The bridge, glued to the top of the instrument (the soundboard), holds one end of the strings. The strings stretch along the neck and over the nut to the head of the instrument. There, tuners hold the other end of the strings and alter their tension to keep them in tune.

A long string vibrates more slowly than a short one and so produces a lower note. That is why a large baritone ukulele has a deeper tone than a soprano ukulele. Each string is tuned to a specific pitch by adjusting the tuner. A tight string or a string that has been shortened by fretting (being held against the fingerboard somewhere along the neck) will produce a higher note when plucked.

The sound of a ukulele starts with a plucked vibrating string, which does not move much air, so its sound is almost inaudible. This is where the body of the instrument comes into play. The strings are attached to the bridge, which is glued to the soundboard. The soundboard vibrates in response to the vibrating strings, producing sound waves that are magnified within the air space in the body and projected through the sound hole.

Idea file. Keep a large notebook like this for sketches, measurements, notes, and full-size tracings of the bodies of ukuleles you admire.

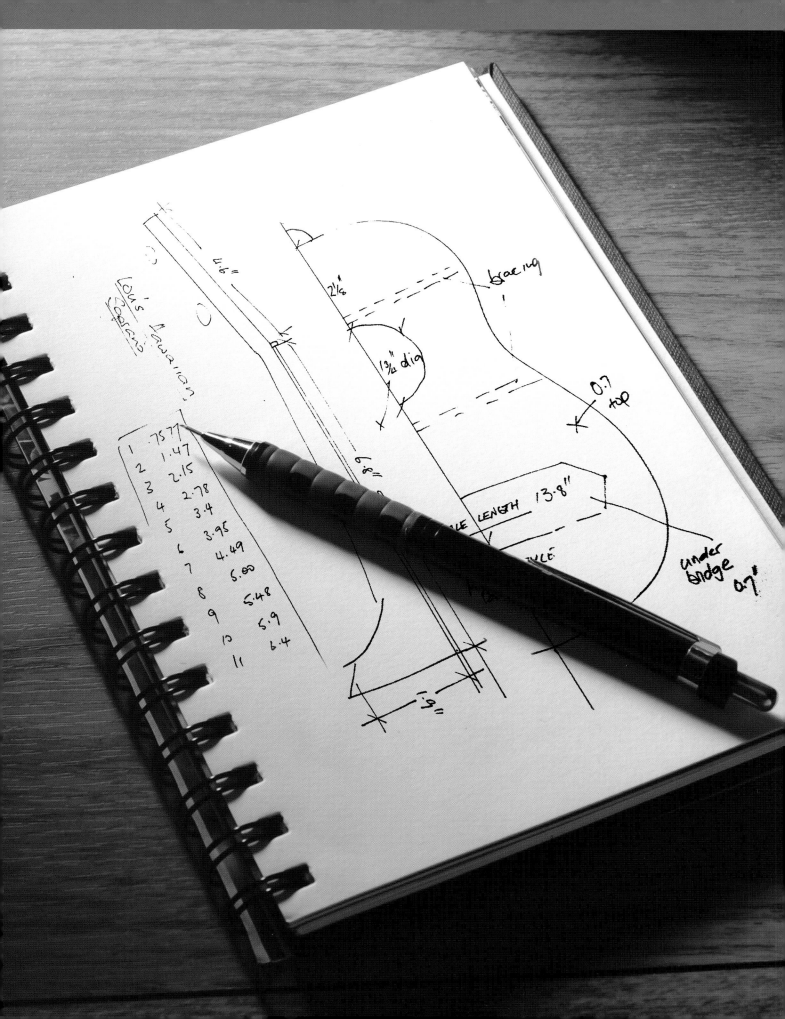

LEARN BY OBSERVING

You can gain a good knowledge of instrument making and design through experience, but you can also learn by critically listening to and examining many ukuleles. Begin your design process by making notes in a notebook or on a large sketchpad, listing all the ukulele designs you like. Trace an outline of the body and add information on the position and size of the sound hole and bridge.

Mount a small piece of mirror on a wire handle so you can look inside at the instrument's bracing pattern and take notes. If a pickup is fitted, examine the mounting, wiring, and output jack. Record the depth of the body, scale length, finish, wood thickness, and bracing details, together with your impressions of the tone. Tap the soundboard with a knuckle and make note of the response.

If you are building a ukulele for someone else, ask them to do some research as well to tell you the size and type of sound that best suits their playing style.

As your knowledge base increases and you become more experienced, you will begin to see patterns emerge from these observations that will guide you in the design process.

Ukulele Fact:

Some seventeen million people attended the Panama-Pacific International Exposition in 1915 and saw the ukulele for the first time.

FACTORS TO CONSIDER

Keep these factors in mind as you study other ukuleles and develop your own designs. No one factor will guarantee that you'll produce either a great-sounding instrument or a dud. Rather, they all play a part in the look of an instrument and, more importantly, how good it sounds.

Size and depth of the body

The scale length of a ukulele will determine its type (soprano, baritone, etc.), while the body usually follows "traditional" proportions, but you can always find exceptions. I have heard some really nice, bright concert and tenor ukuleles with bodies only about 1¾" (44mm) deep. I once built an instrument for a client who wanted a soprano ukulele, but with a longer scale length and wide fingerboard to accommodate his large fingers.

Shape of the body

The traditional curved shape separates the soundboard into two sections on either side of the sound hole. The smaller section at the neck amplifies the high frequencies, leaving the bottom end to handle the bass. However, some makers can produce a fine-sounding ukulele with unconventional body shapes. See the gallery, pages 12–31, for some examples.

Type of wood used for the body

Be guided by Chapter 2, page 36, which covers wood and wood selection for the body and soundboard of a ukulele.

Thickness of the wood

The wood I use for the body is about 5/64"–3/32" (1.9–2.5mm) thick, which yields a bright sound. Larger ukuleles have a higher string tension and therefore require more bracing on the soundboard. Be guided by the observations in your notebook.

Size of the sound hole

A larger sound hole will reduce the tension on the soundboard and produce a deeper tone. Listen for the variations in tone when you are examining ukuleles.

Bridge construction

Keep the bridge small and light. A bridge with thin wings at each end spreads the pressure applied by the tightened strings and requires less bracing under the soundboard.

Bracing pattern

A traditional Martin-style soprano ukulele (named for the major guitar manufacturer Martin & Co.) has two lateral braces on either side of the sound hole. As the plan on page 57 shows, my design uses two more braces to keep the soundboard from warping under the tension of the strings You need to design bracing based on your observations and then tune the bracing for the optimum sound.

Type of finish

A ukulele with a heavy gloss finish will produce a different sound from one that has a light oil finish.

Type of strings

There are two types of strings: hard, bright-sounding strings (Aquila Nylgut is the major brand) and soft-sounding brown or black nylon or fluorocarbon strings (GHS and Worth are the principal brands). Ukuleles traditionally have a high G string, but it is sometimes replaced with a heavier string that is tuned one octave lower.

M. Nunes: Inventor of the Ukulele

Manuel Nunes, one of the earliest-known manufacturers of the ukulele, arrived in Hawaii in 1879. Nunes worked as a plantation hand and later as a cabinetmaker. His woodworking skills allowed him to produce musical instruments, and he was eventually labeled a guitar maker. His ukulele manufacturing company, M. Nunes and Sons, was founded in 1910, and Nunes began to refer to himself as the inventor of the original ukulele. Most of his ukuleles were labeled "M. Nunes, Inventor of the Ukulele and Taro Patch Fiddles in Honolulu in 1879." Nunes would pass his skills on to his sons, and to individuals like Sam Kamaka, who would later start his own ukulele manufacturing company.

CHAPTER 2

How to Choose the Right Wood

If you have the time to search through the racks at cabinet-making supply stores, lumberyards, and sawmills, you may well find some great wood at very low prices. However, you can also find good supplies of quality wood via the Internet. Suppliers select suitable wood for its appearance and tonal qualities, milling it close to final thickness so it only needs to be sanded to size. This tonewood is often supplied in matching sets for a particular size of ukulele: front, back, and two sides. Some sets include a neck blank. You can expand the range and type of wood available for your ukulele projects by selecting guitar wood blanks and cutting them down to make more than one ukulele.

You do not need much wood to make a ukulele. So, for the best results when making your first ukulele, select the very best wood you can afford, treat it as precious, and work to that level of excellence.

If you go to local suppliers, hunt around for scrap pieces and boards that were rejected because they were too figured. These are gems to a luthier. A book-matched front or back for a soprano ukulele can be cut from a board 3½" (89mm) wide, which can easily be recut on a band saw or table saw. Some book-matched sets are spectacular and are typically found on the backs of expensive instruments.

When buying wood online, be wary of auctions and look for established suppliers with a reputation to maintain. You will find a list of suppliers I have used in the back of the book. You can often find information and comments about a particular supplier by searching the instrument-making forums on the Internet. (See Information and Resources, page 92.) You can also discuss your project with other builders, gaining information and moral support when you need it.

If you can select wood in person, look for pieces that have a tight, quartersawn grain with no knots and no apparent defects or wandering grain lines. If you are looking for figured wood from a local supplier, bring along a block plane and a bottle of water or mineral spirits with you. With the seller's permission, plane a small area of a board, then douse it to make the grain and figure pop.

One of a kind. Highly figured woods, like the koa wood used to make this concert ukulele, can give your instrument a unique touch. Look for distinctive pieces when selecting wood for your instrument. Ukulele made by John Ramsey of Palm Tree Ukuleles, Colorado.

Work through the samples, tapping the wood with your knuckle. The tone will vary from a dull clunk to a nice bright resonance. Thinner wood samples will have a higher pitch, which is not to be confused with better tone. Over time, you will learn to select wood with a nice, bright tone, but for now, let your supplier and your intuition guide you.

Thin pieces of wood respond rapidly to changes in the humidity of the workshop and will curl out of shape, so keep them stored between two sheets of plywood or wrap them in plastic to reduce warping.

Keep in mind that the sanding dust of some species of wood may irritate the skin, eyes, and bronchial tubes. Play it safe. Wear a dust mask approved by a safety organization like the National Institute for Occupational Safety and Health and install an effective dust collection system in your shop.

Ukulele Fact:

Many United States soldiers returning from the South Pacific after WWII brought ukuleles home with them.

UNDERSTANDING WOOD GRADES

Wood is sold by description and grade. Online retailers often provide photographs of a typical sample, which is useful when you want highly figured wood.

Wood for musical instruments is graded with a system of *A*s. The more *A*s assigned to a piece of wood, the higher the grade (and the higher the price).

AAAA grade. Sometimes referred to as master grade, this is the top wood grade available. It is often highly figured with spectacular grain, and goes by all sorts of exotic names, including bearclaw, figured, flamed, fiddleback, curly, and the like. It is best to buy this grade of figured wood after viewing a typical sample photograph.

AAAA spruce and cedar. Spruce and cedar are very stiff woods, typically used for soundboards. They have a bright tone when tapped. AAAA is the top grade for spruce and cedar, denoting wood that is quartersawn, with a grain count of more than twenty lines per inch (25mm), evenly spaced, and with even coloring.

AAA grade. This identifies wood with straight, tight grain and good tone, but with less figure than AAAA wood. AAA grade makes excellent ukuleles.

AAA spruce. Wood meeting this grade is quartersawn, similar to AAAA spruce and cedar, but with a grain count up to fifteen lines per inch (25mm). The wood has no color variation and is stiff, with a good, bright tap tone.

AA grade. This is low-quality wood, not worth buying if you plan to spend hours making a ukulele.

Practice grade. As its name implies, this inexpensive wood is useful for beginners to use to practice various construction techniques.

GOOD WOODS FOR UKULELES

Ukuleles can be made from any of the countless wood varieties available throughout the world, but just because a wood is aesthetically appealing does not mean it will produce an instrument with a quality sound. The type of wood you use will help determine the sound and tone of your ukulele. Here are some wood varieties that are good for producing a quality instrument.

African blackwood (*Dalbergia melanoxylon*). Color varies from purplish black to dark brown with black streaks. Like koa and Australian blackwood, this wood has an excellent tap tone.

Australian blackwood (*Acacia melanoxylon*). The Australian blackwood tree is almost a twin to the Hawaiian koa tree and makes a great-sounding ukulele. The wood is slightly lighter than koa, with narrow bands of darker growth rings. There are also highly figured samples available at premium prices.

Hawaiian koa wood (*Acacia koa*). This traditional ukulele wood has a golden-brown color with dark streaks. Some prized samples have a curly or flamed figure. A favorite with ukulele makers, koa wood will produce a nice balanced tone with a bright treble.

Mahogany (genus *Meliaceae*). Reddish-brown color with straight grain and excellent warm tonal qualities. Mahogany is a Native American word for genuine American mahogany, which is rare. Other types of wood are often used in place of American mahogany because of their similarity in appearance and tone. These include Khaya (African mahogany) and Toona (Chinese mahogany). Other species of wood are sold as mahogany because of their similarity in appearance, but they lack a good tone.

Mango (*Anacardiaceae mangifera*). This blond wood often shows highly figured grain and coloring. The reasonably coarse grain and texture produces a soft, mellow tone.

Rosewood (genus *Dalbergia*). Dark-colored hardwood with good tonal qualities.

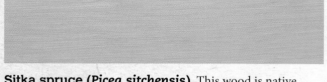

Sitka spruce (*Picea sitchensis*). This wood is native to Alaska and northwest Canada. Sitka spruce is used for soundboards in most acoustic guitars because of its consistent quality and bright sound; those same qualities add volume to a ukulele.

Western red cedar (*Thuja plicata*). This species comes from western Canada and the Pacific Northwest of the United States. The color ranges from light tan to a very dark reddish-brown. When used for a soundboard, it produces a mellow tone and is best suited to the larger-bodied ukuleles.

The Beauty of Koa

Ukuleles made from koa wood are some of the most prized and expensive versions of the instrument. The koa tree is only native to Hawaii, and countless generations of Hawaiians have used its wood to build canoes and other necessities. The tree grows incredibly fast, gaining up to an inch (25mm) in diameter every year, and easily reaching a height of 100 feet (30m). The wood has a red hue and a unique curly grain pattern. It looks exceptional when treated with oil or varnish and is treasured today as one of the most beautiful woods in the world.

PHOTO BY KEITH OGATA.

PD-3. The soundboard of this ukulele perfectly demonstrates how koa can be used to enhance an instrument's appearance. Ukulele created by Keith Ogata.

Make Your Own Ukulele How to Choose the Right Wood

Make the most of grain. When you select your own tonewood, you can look for boards with great grain or figure and cut pieces that match like facing pages in a book. Shown here are book-matched pieces of sassafras.

CHAPTER 3

Build the Boxer

You can make this simple soprano ukulele with hand tools and a cordless drill, using plywood for the box, pine for the neck, and hardwood for the rest. An electric detail sander, though not essential, will make the project even easier. There's no wood bending involved in making the body. You rough-cut the neck with a handsaw and give it its final shape with a rasp and sandpaper. Fitting the frets, the nut, and the bridge is the same as it would be for any other ukulele.

The Kamaka Story

Kamaka Hawaii, Inc. began as a one-man company in the early 1900s when Sam Kamaka started making ukuleles in his Hawaiian home. In 1916, Kamaka Ukulele and Guitar Works was established, followed by Kamaka Ukulele in 1921. Kamaka developed the pineapple ukulele, creating the pattern for the oval-shaped instrument in the mid-1920s. The unique design produced a distinct sound, setting it apart from the traditional "figure eight" ukulele, rich and warm. Sam Kamaka died in 1953, and the business passed into the hands of his sons, Sam Jr. and Fred. Kamaka's sons have had just as much success making ukuleles as their father, renaming the company Kamaka Hawaii, Inc. in 1968. Today, Kamaka's grandsons also play a significant role in running the company, which celebrated its ninetieth anniversary in 2006.

The Boxer. The boxy shape makes this ukulele easy to build. It has a nice soprano tone.

Tools

- » Ruler or tape measure
- » Compass
- » Miter box and saw
- » Coping saw with assorted blades
- » A Japanese backsaw or fretsaw with a 0.023" (0.6mm) kerf
- » Ripsaw

- » Cordless drill
- » Wood rasp
- » File
- » Clamps
- » Clamping weights (a brick wrapped in duct tape or heavy exercise weights)

- » Bench vise
- » Hammer
- » Sandpaper, from P100 to P400 grit
- » Double-sided tape
- » Spray lacquer or oil-based finish

Materials

Part	Qty.	Material	Dimensions (L x W x D)
Top	1	Plywood	10" x 7" x ³⁄₃₂" (254 x 178 x 2.5mm)
Bottom	1	Plywood	10" x 7" x ³⁄₃₂" (254 x 178 x 2.5mm)
Box sides	1 (later cut into 4 pieces)	Cedar or similar stable wood	36" x 2" x ³⁄₈" (914 x 51 x 10mm)
Neck	1	Clear pine or fir	13" x 3" x 1½" (330 x 76 x 38mm)
Bracing	2	Hardwood	18" x ³⁄₁₆" x ³⁄₈" (457 x 5 x 10mm)
Fingerboard	1	Hardwood	8" x 2" x ³⁄₁₆" (203 x 51 x 5mm)
Bridge	1	Hardwood	2¼" x ¼" x ⁵⁄₈" (57 x 6 x 16mm)
Bridge plate	1	Plywood	2" (51mm)
Neck block	1	Pine	2" x ¾" (51 x 19mm)
End block	1	Pine	1" x ¾" (25 x 19mm)
Fretwire	1		24" (610mm)
Tuners	4		Purchase from a luthier supplier like Stewart MacDonald (*www.stewmac.com*)
Nut	1	Bone or plastic	Purchase from a luthier supplier like Stewart MacDonald (*www.stewmac.com*)

Ukulele Fact:

The *machete* was Madeira's national instrument long before it rose to popularity as the ukulele.

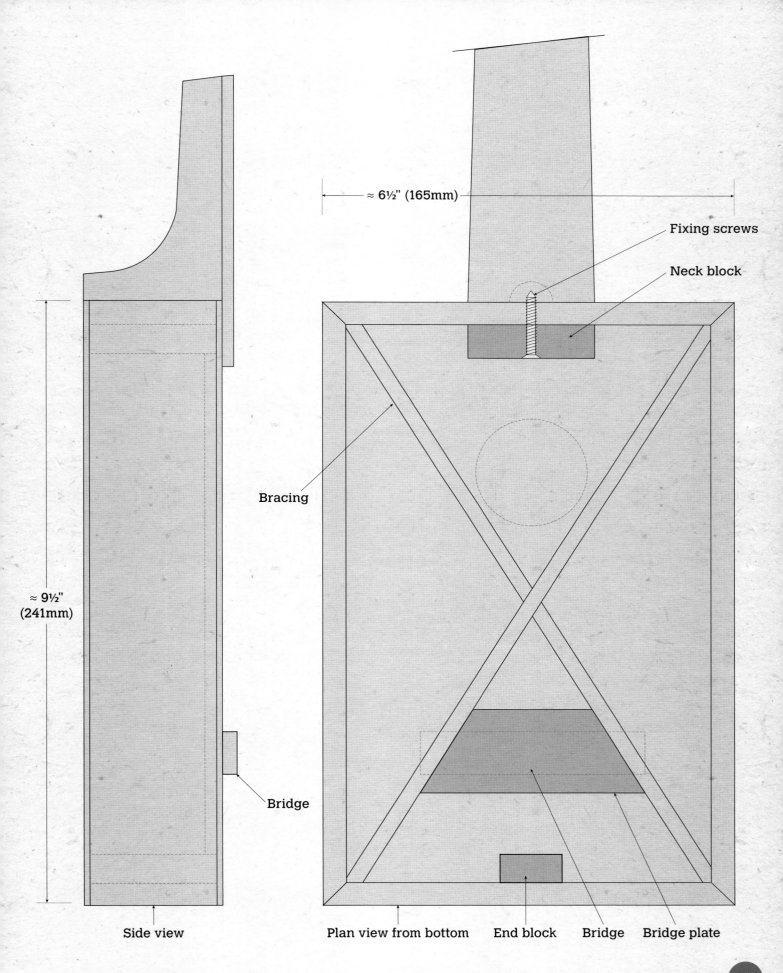

≈ 6½" (165mm)

Fixing screws

Neck block

Bracing

≈ 9½"
(241mm)

Bridge

Side view

Plan view from bottom

End block

Bridge

Bridge plate

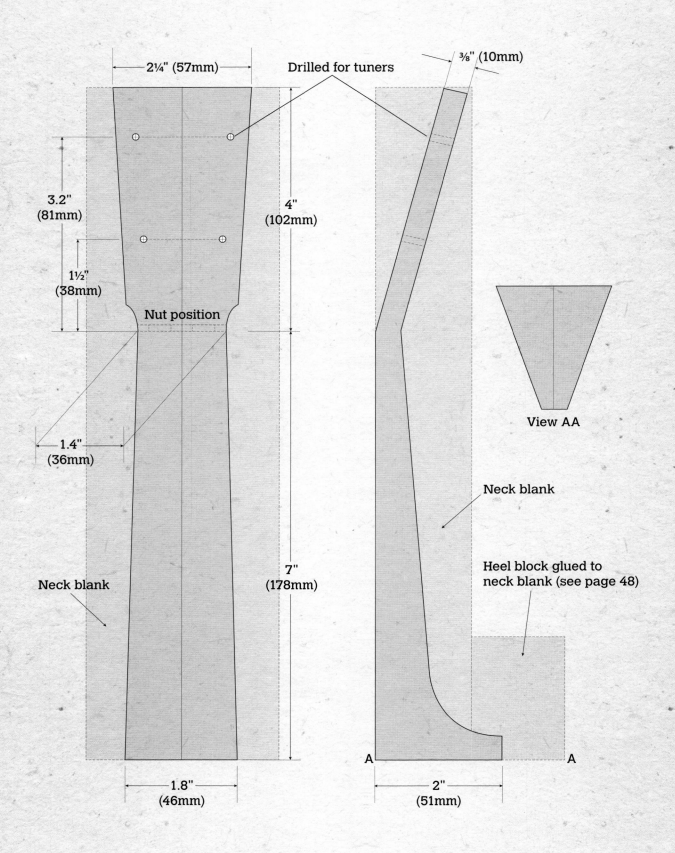

2¼" (57mm)

Drilled for tuners

⅜" (10mm)

3.2" (81mm)

4" (102mm)

1½" (38mm)

Nut position

1.4" (36mm)

View AA

Neck blank

7" (178mm)

Heel block glued to neck blank (see page 48)

Neck blank

1.8" (46mm)

2" (51mm)

A   A

MAKE THE BOX

If you have a cigar box, use it and proceed with the bracing and fitting as described on page 48. Otherwise, begin by following the steps below.

1. **Cut the sides.** Take the wood piece you selected for the ukulele's sides and cut the four pieces you need to rough length. Then, use the miter box to cut them to the exact size, mitering the ends at a 45-degree angle. Be sure the opposing sides are exactly the same length. Set up a clamping system by tying a cord or strap around the assembled sides, and then tighten it by inserting scraps of wood between the box and the strap. The scrap blocks add tension to press the joints together. Use a check stick (see photo) or tape measure to ensure the diagonal measurements are equal. This tells you the box is square.

2. **Glue the sides together.** Check that the four sides sit evenly on a flat surface and there are no gaps in the corner joints. Double check the length of the pieces and re-cut the miter joints if necessary. When everything looks all right, glue the pieces together and clamp them again. When the glue has set, check to see that the tops and bottoms of the pieces are flush at the corner joints. If necessary, sand the pieces flush with 100-grit sandpaper wrapped around a block. To keep the edge square, sand across two pieces at once.

3. **Cut the top and bottom pieces.** Choose the best-looking plywood for the top, or soundboard. Find the best face and, on the opposite side, trace the inside and outside of the body (you should wait until the glue holding the body together is completely dry before you do this). Also draw lines to indicate the diagonal bracing and a circle for the sound hole. The sound hole should be 1¾" (44mm) in diameter and its edges located ⅜" (10mm) from each brace. Cut the plywood, leaving 1/16" (2mm) extra space around the edges. Cut an identical piece for the back.

4. **Cut the sound hole.** Drill a pilot hole and cut out the sound hole with a coping saw. Sand the edge smooth and be sure the curve is uniform.

An Orchestra with Attitude

The Ukulele Orchestra of Great Britain is an eight-person group, formed in 1985, that performs around the world using only ukuleles and their voices—no other instrumentation is to be found. The orchestra's concerts are fun and entertaining, pulling from all genres of music for performance material. You can expect to hear classical pieces followed immediately by rock anthems. The orchestra's notoriety and unique performance style has led to concerts all over the world, including venues like Royal Albert Hall in London and Carnegie Hall in New York.

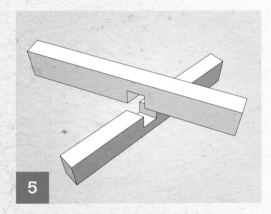

5

5. Fit the braces. Cut the braces to fit and taper their ends. Fit each brace in position in the body. Mark where the two braces intersect and cut a half-lap joint in them at the intersection. The identical notches in the braces will allow them to overlap to support the ukulele.

6. Attach the soundboard. Glue the soundboard to the ukulele body by placing the soundboard upside down on a flat surface. Apply glue to the top edges of the ukulele body, and then place the body (glue side down) over the soundboard. Use your tracing on the soundboard to align the body. Hold the body in place with a weight until the glue dries.

7. Sand and attach the bridge plate and end blocks. Sand the edge of the soundboard flush with the box sides, and then glue in the end blocks and bracing. Measure and cut the bridge plate from plywood or a thin scrap of hardwood. Glue it in between the bracing, so it will be under the bridge. The end blocks provide extra support for screws, and the bridge plate helps support the bridge when it is placed on the soundboard.

MAKE THE NECK

7

8. Make the neck blank. You can make a thick neck blank from thin stock. Say you have wood boards that are 1" (25mm) thick, but you need a blank of twice that thickness. As the drawing shows, take a tapered offcut and glue it to the underside of the head to make it the correct thickness. Glue a block at the other end at the neck joint. For this project, select a knot-free piece of pine or fir with 13" x 3" x 1½" (330 x 76 x 38mm) dimensions. Cut a 2" (51mm) piece from one end and glue it to the bottom of the original piece, making it 3" (76mm) thick where the neck will join the body. Square off this end so that the neck will align perfectly with the body. Now use the plan to draw the shape of the neck on the blank.

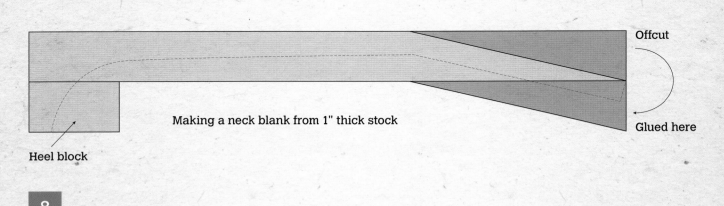

Offcut

Making a neck blank from 1" thick stock

Heel block

Glued here

8

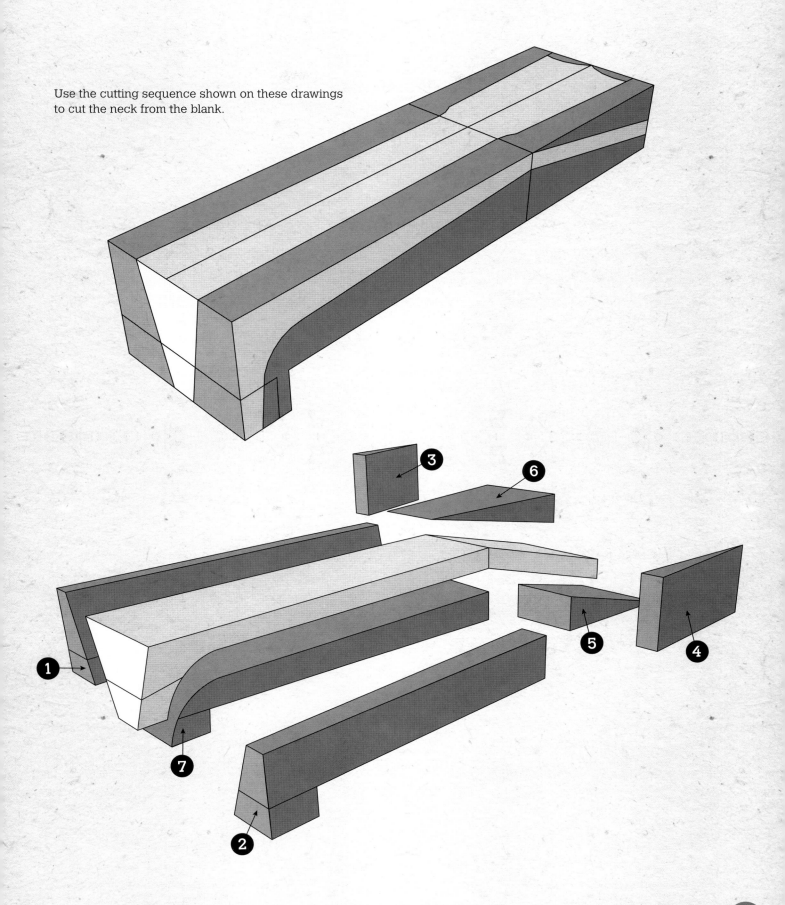

Use the cutting sequence shown on these drawings to cut the neck from the blank.

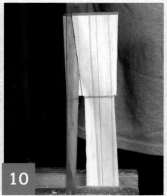

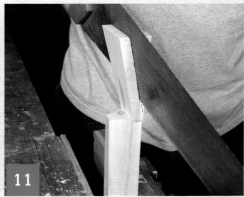

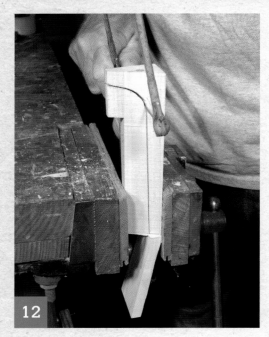

9. **Make the first set of neck cuts.** Follow the cutting sequence shown in the drawings on page 49 to rough out the neck. Begin by placing the blank in a vise and using a rip saw to cut with the grain along the length of the neck to the nut position. Saw in from the side to remove the waste.

10. **Make the second set of neck cuts.** Using the ripsaw, make angled cuts to define the shape of the head.

11. **Shape the head of the neck.** Use the rip saw to make two cuts, sawing the back of the head and then the face to give it the angled shape you want.

12. **Make the final cut.** Use a coping saw to make a curved cut down the back of the neck to narrow it and remove any excess wood.

13. **Complete the final shaping.** Carefully shape the finished neck by clamping a 2x4 (38 x 89mm) in a vise and attach the neck to it upside down, using double-sided tape to hold it fast. Begin with a rasp and shape the neck roughly to size. Sight along the neck and feel the profile with your hands to be sure it remains symmetrical as you refine its shape.

14. **Sand the neck and drill tuner holes.** Sand the neck, beginning with P100-grit sandpaper and working through the grits to P220. Be sure you remove any sanding scratches with the next grade. If you are using a detail sander, coarse, medium, and fine grades will do the job. Mark and drill holes to fit the tuners.

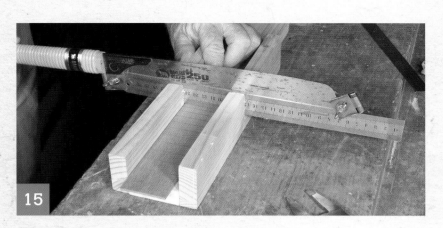

MAKE THE FINGERBOARD

15. Cut the fret slots. Use the miter box to square off one end of the fingerboard blank. Then, measure and mark the fret positions using the chart below. Cut right-angled slots in the sides to guide the saw. Check the depth required for your fretwire and saw the fret slots with the Japanese saw or fretsaw. Clamp a ruler onto the saw to serve as a depth stop. To ensure these cuts are uniform, make the jig shown in the photo and use it to guide the saw.

16. Shape the fingerboard. Center the fingerboard on the finished neck and trace the shape of the neck on the underside of the fingerboard. Saw the fingerboard to shape, position it on the neck with double-sided tape, and sand the edges flush with the neck.

13.97" (355mm) Fret Scale

Fret number	Distance from nut	Distance between frets
1	0.784" (20mm)	Nut–fret 1: 0.784" (20mm)
2	1.524" (39mm)	Fret 1–2: 0.740" (19mm)
3	2.223" (56mm)	Fret 2–3: 0.699" (18mm)
4	2.882" (73mm)	Fret 3–4: 0.659" (17mm)
5	3.504" (89mm)	Fret 4–5: 0.622" (16mm)
6	4.092" (104mm)	Fret 5–6: 0.588" (15mm)
7	4.646" (118mm)	Fret 6–7: 0.544" (14mm)
8	5.169" (131mm)	Fret 7–8: 0.523" (13mm)
9	5.663" (144mm)	Fret 8–9: 0.494" (13mm)
10	6.130" (156mm)	Fret 9–10: 0.467" (12mm)
11	6.570" (167mm)	Fret 10–11: 0.440" (11mm)
12	6.985" (177mm)	Fret 11–12: 0.415" (11mm)

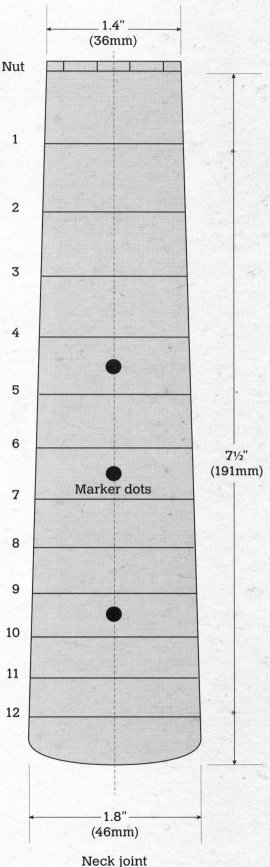

1.4" (36mm)

Nut

1

2

3

4

5

6

Marker dots

7

8

9

10

11

12

7½" (191mm)

1.8" (46mm)

Neck joint

ASSEMBLY

17. Install the frets. Remove the fingerboard and fit the frets. Starting at the fret closest to the nut, cut the fretwire to length and lightly tap it into position. Check that it is aligned at 90 degrees to the fingerboard. Place a scrap of hardwood over the fretwire and seat it with one sharp tap of a hammer. When all the fretwire is in place, file the edges flush and round them over.

18. Attach the neck. Align the neck and body face down on a flat surface. Drill a hole from inside the body into the neck. Wrap tape on the drill bit to indicate where to stop drilling if you're concerned about drilling too deeply. This will form two holes, one in the body and one in the neck. Glue the neck in place, making sure the drilled holes are aligned. Secure the neck with a screw. Be sure the screw is short so it doesn't protrude through the neck.

19. Attach the fingerboard. Glue the fingerboard in position on the neck, using rubber bands for clamps.

20. Attach the back to the body. Glue and clamp the back in place, weighing it down until the glue dries. Sand the edges flush with the body, as you did when you glued the soundboard in place.

MAKE AND ATTACH THE BRIDGE AND NUT

You can buy a ready-made bridge and nut from a luthier supplier, but neither piece is very difficult to make.

21. Make the bridge. For the bridge, refer to the plan on page 58. Cut a piece of hardwood to size and round over the top edges. Mark the position of the slots in the rear of the bridge. Clamp a piece of scrap to the bottom face, flush with the rear edge. Drill four ³⁄₁₆" (5mm)-diameter shallow holes on the seam where the two pieces meet. This produces half-circle slots for the string knots. Remove the scrap and use a coping saw to cut four slots in the rear edge to take the strings. Use the Japanese saw or fretsaw to cut a slot across the top. Fit a piece of fretwire in the slot and file the edges flush with the end of the bridge.

22. Make the nut. Use a file and follow the plan on page 58 to mark string positions. Make four shallow cuts with the fretsaw to mark the position of strings. Glue the nut in position with cyanoacrylate adhesive.

23. Finish the string slots in the nut. Use a coping saw blade that is slightly wider than each of the strings. Place a 0.05" (1.3mm) cardboard shim across the fingerboard directly below the nut. (The cardboard from the back of a pad of paper is about right.) Cut the slots in the nut down to this shim. This will give you approximately 0.03" (0.8mm) string clearance. Shape each slot, making one cut parallel to the fingerboard, then angle the saw down so it is parallel with the head and pointed toward the appropriate tuner and complete the cut.

24. Mark the scale length. Starting from the inside face of the nut, measure the scale length (the distance from the front edge of the nut to where the strings contact the bridge) and draw a light line on the soundboard at a right angle to the neck. This line marks the position of the saddle of the bridge.

25. Align and attach the bridge, sand, and finish. Using a straightedge extended along each side of the fingerboard, draw a line along the straightedge where it intersects with the bridge line. This will give you the correct scale length and alignment for the bridge. Glue the bridge and clamp it in position with a light weight. Now you can do the final sanding and apply a finish to your new ukulele.

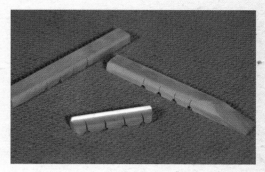

Various examples of bridge construction.

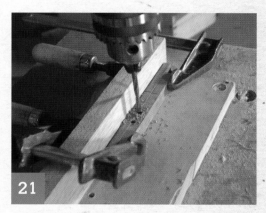

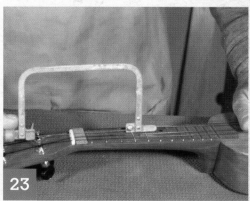

CHAPTER 4

Build a Professional-Grade Ukulele

This project will make you a luthier. You will learn all the steps involved in making a stringed instrument: thicknessing the wood for the soundboard, bending the wood for the body sides, making your own rope binding for the seam where the top joins the sides, and all the steps that go into creating the neck and fingerboard. You will also learn a thing or two about giving the ukulele a smooth, professional finish.

When I made my first ukulele, I decided I wanted to have an easy time of it. So, like this chapter, I broke the construction process down into simple steps and tackled one step at a time. Whenever I encountered something unfamiliar, I took a piece of scrap and practiced until I gained enough confidence to proceed. I stopped work or went for a bike ride whenever I got frustrated or flustered. The job was invariably easier the next day, and I decided that if I made a mistake that couldn't be fixed, then it wasn't a mistake at all, but part of the learning process.

Ukulele Fact:

Portuguese immigrants also took the ukulele to places like Cape Town, the Antilles, Asia, and South America.

A professional-grade instrument. The instructions in this chapter will show you how to build this soprano ukulele, complete with traditional rope binding around the soundboard.

Tools

» Table saw fitted with a fine-tooth blade and a crosscut sled

» Band saw with a ½" (13mm), 4 teeth per inch (4 teeth per 25mm) blade and ¼" (6mm), 6 teeth per inch blade

» Japanese backsaw or fretsaw with a 0.023" (0.6mm) kerf

» Drill press

» Vernier or dial calipers

» Electric bending iron or shop-made gas-heated bending iron

» Bending strap

» Random-orbit sander with P100-, P180-, and P220-grit discs

» A rubber circular sanding disc for the drill press with coarse and medium sanding discs

» Hand plane

» Coarse and fine wood rasps

» Fine metal file

» Cabinet scraper

» Nut files or a series of fine saw blades from a coping saw kit

» Router

» Optional router table

» Cordless drill/screwdriver

» Clamps, including 2 bar clamps

» Large rubber bands and clothespins for clamping

» Combination square, ruler, and tape measure

» Aliphatic resin glue such as Titebond

» Epoxy adhesive

» Cyanoacrylate adhesive

» Sandpaper ranging from P150 through P800 grits

» Aerosol instrument lacquer or nitrocellulose lacquer and spray equipment

Materials

Part	Qty.	Material	Dimensions (L x W x D)
Top	1	Hardwood	10" x 7" x 0.09" (254 x 178 x 2mm)
Bottom	1	Hardwood	10" x 7" x 0.09" (254 x 178 x 2mm)
Sides	2	Hardwood	15" x 2½" x 0.07" (381 x 64 x 2mm)
Neck	1	Hardwood	12" x 2½" x 1" (305 x 64 x 25mm)
Bridge	1	Hardwood	2¼" x ⅝" x ¼" (57 x 16 x 6mm)
Bracing	2	Hardwood	18" x ⅜" x 3⁄16" (457 x 10 x 5mm)
Neck and heel blocks	2	Hardwood	2" x 1½" (51 x 38mm)
Fingerboard	1	Hardwood	8" x 2" x 0.09" (203 x 51 x 2mm)
Body jig	1	Medium-density fiberboard	96" x 48" x ¾" (2438 x 1219 x 19mm)
Fretwire	1		24" (610mm)
Tuners	4		Purchase from a luthier supplier like Stewart MacDonald (www.stewmac.com)
Nut	1	Bone or plastic	Purchase from a luthier supplier like Stewart MacDonald (www.stewmac.com)

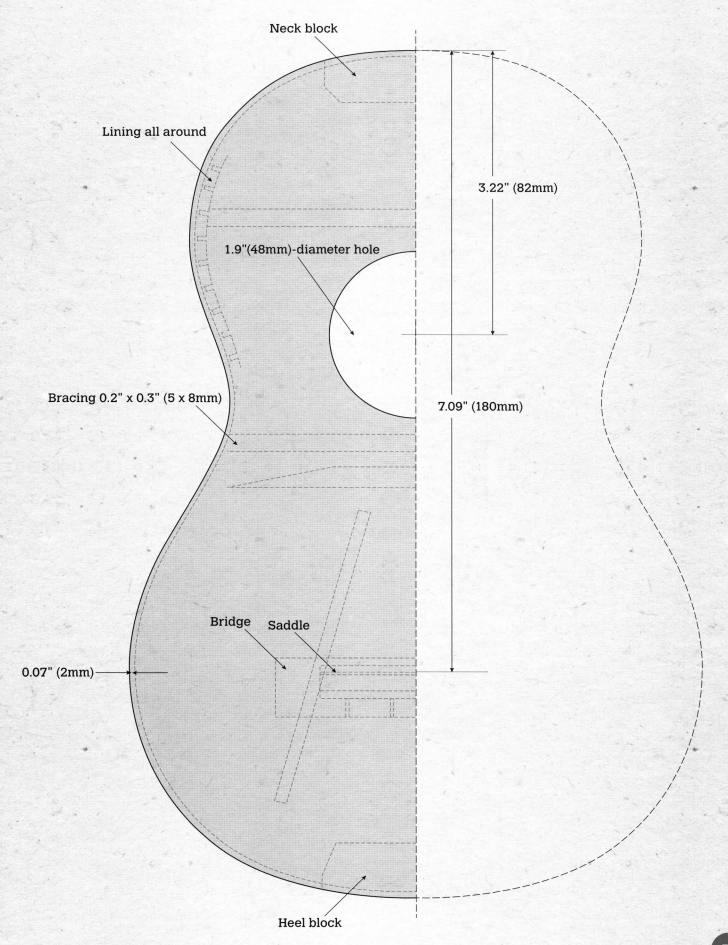

Neck block

Lining all around

1.9"(48mm)-diameter hole

3.22" (82mm)

Bracing 0.2" x 0.3" (5 x 8mm)

7.09" (180mm)

Bridge   Saddle

0.07" (2mm)

Heel block

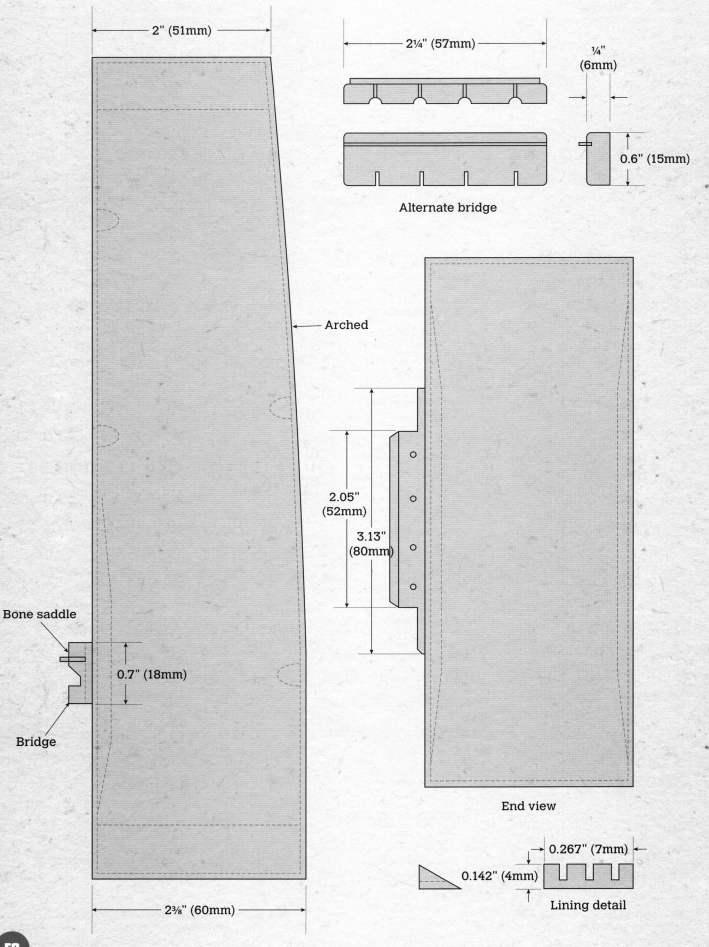

2" (51mm)

2¼" (57mm)

¼" (6mm)

0.6" (15mm)

Alternate bridge

Arched

2.05" (52mm)

3.13" (80mm)

Bone saddle

0.7" (18mm)

Bridge

End view

0.267" (7mm)

0.142" (4mm)

Lining detail

2⅜" (60mm)

58

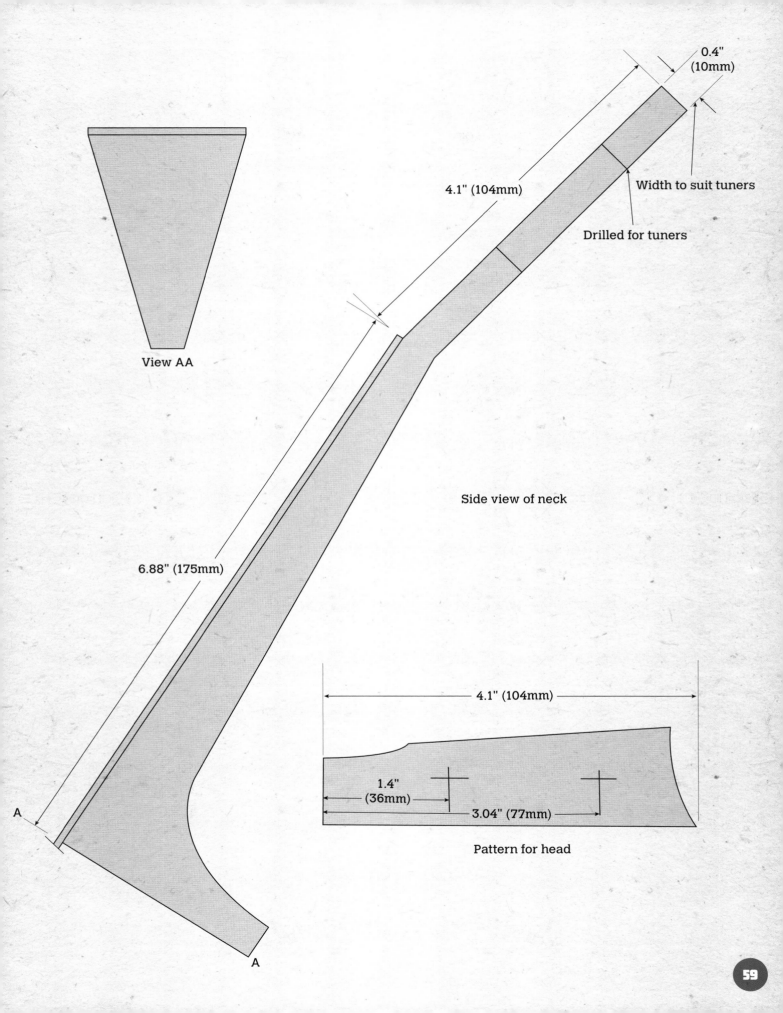

View AA

0.4" (10mm)

Width to suit tuners

4.1" (104mm)

Drilled for tuners

Side view of neck

6.88" (175mm)

A

A

4.1" (104mm)

1.4" (36mm)

3.04" (77mm)

Pattern for head

THICKNESS THE TONEWOOD

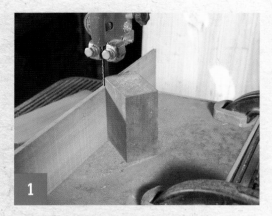

If you are using wood from a kit, the tonewood is probably very close to its final thickness, and you can skip to page 62. If you are working with rough lumber, joint one face and edge and resaw the board to a thickness of ³⁄₁₆" (5mm). You can do that on a band saw or a table saw. The wood will then be ready for sanding to its final thickness.

1. **Resaw the wood.** To resaw on the band saw, use a ½" (13mm) blade with 3 or 4 teeth per inch (25mm). If need be, check the owner's manual to be sure the blade is properly tensioned. Make a tall fence from plywood or medium-density fiberboard and set it to compensate for blade drift. Hold the smooth face of the stock against the fence and feed the wood through slowly. If you hear the motor slow and begin to labor, slow the feed rate. Make sure you cut the wood to be slightly thicker than what you need so you can carefully plane and sand it to thickness. If you need to cut more than one piece of tonewood from the same blank, joint the newly sawn face on the blank before running the wood through the band saw again. Cut pieces for the soundboard, sides, and back of the instrument.

To resaw on the table saw, use an anti-kickback ripping blade and a zero-clearance throat plate fitted with a splitter. Position the rip fence so the offcut is on the opposite side of the blade from the fence, to minimize the risk of kickback. (I can tell you from experience, a narrow piece of hardwood that kicks back can inflict a serious injury and keep you from playing a ukulele for quite a while.) Set the blade depth to a little more than half the width of the board, cut along the length, and then flip the wood end for end and cut again. Joint the face, reposition the rip fence, and make additional cuts until you have all the tonewood you need.

2. **Remove marks and bring to final thickness.** To remove saw marks and give the wood a nice even finish, use a drum sander or a hand plane. Avoid using a portable belt sander, which is likely to leave an uneven surface, or a random-orbit sander, which is really only suited for fine surface sanding. A hand plane works well for thicknessing straight-grained wood, but may tear out the grain on heavily figured wood. I use a Stanley #4 honed to a keen edge and with a heavy-duty cap iron.

I've found that the following method works well for planing a piece of tonewood. Use bench dogs to hold it in place, and score the entire surface with a coarse wood rasp. Plane to remove the score lines. Work carefully and repeat the scoring and planing until you reach the desired thickness.

Sometimes the cheapest and easiest way to thickness a board is to pay a local cabinetmaker to do the work. When you specify the finished thickness, allow a whisker for your own finish sanding, but if you own a lathe, you can build a fixture to use it as a drum sander. See the sidebar at the right to learn how.

Ukulele Tip:

Only polish the body of your ukulele; don't touch the strings.

Make a Sander for Your Lathe

You can easily convert a wood lathe to a drum sander with an adjustable table. Make the drum from a 12" (305mm) length of pipe 4" (102mm) in diameter, such as a steam pipe or an aluminum irrigation pipe fitted with turned wood end plugs.

To make the plugs, glue together two square pieces of framing lumber face to face, with a sheet of brown paper (like a piece cut from a grocery bag) in the glue joint. The paper makes it easy to separate the two pieces. Center and screw one side to the faceplate. Chuck a ¾" (19mm)-diameter Forstner bit in the tailstock and drill a shallow hole. Use epoxy to bed a small nut in the hole, so it is flush with the wood surface. Cover it with plastic and bring the tailstock center up to the nut and allow the glue to set. Turn the wood to the internal diameter of the pipe, tapering the wood slightly from both ends toward the center. Use a chisel to separate the halves of the plug at the glue line and fit the two halves to the pipe. Drive screws through the pipe to hold the plugs in place. Leave the drive end screwed to the faceplate and bring the tailstock into position against the nut to ensure that the pipe runs on axis.

Cover the drum with ½" (13mm)-thick high-density foam; a camping mattress from a sporting goods store works well. Cut it to size and attach it to the drum with contact cement.

Spiral-wind a strip of cloth-backed sandpaper to the drum and tape down both ends; 100-grit paper is a good all-purpose grade. Trim the paper square to the ends of the drum.

Make the sander table from a piece of ¾" (19mm) medium-density fiberboard, hinged to a base that is

Shop-made but effective. A metal pipe with turned plugs in either end converts a lathe into a very useful thickness sander. An auto jack beneath the base lets you fine-tune the amount of material sanded away in each pass.

clamped to the lathe bed. Use an auto jack to adjust the table. Do not lubricate the surface of the table with silicone or wax, because it may contaminate the wood and interfere with the final lacquer finish.

Finally, fit the sander with an effective dust-extraction system. Mine, shown in the photo, uses a length of PVC pipe with a 1" (25mm) slot that is positioned over the drum and connected to the shop's dust-collection system. The narrow slot provides high-velocity suction. You can add a skirt to the rear of the pipe to channel the dust into the system.

Raise the table as needed. Set the lathe speed for 700 revolutions per minute (rpm) and use a push stick to feed the wood into the drum once it is up to speed. Rather than try to do all the sanding in one pass, make multiple light passes until you reach the desired thickness. Feeling tired? Leave the sanding until the next day.

MAKE THE FRONT AND BACK PANELS

You can make the front and back panels from one board or two. Two-piece panels allow you to use narrow stock and create opportunities for spectacular bookmatched panels.

To join the thin wood panels, you must have a perfect seam between the two pieces. The simplest way to create the seam is with a hand plane and an improvised shooting board.

3. Plane the edges. Clamp a length of wood at the edge of the bench. It should be about 24" x 3" x ¾" (610 x 76 x 19mm). As the photo shows, hold the plane on its side with the sole against the edge of the board as you push the wood past the blade. Hone the blade and set it to take very fine shavings. For the best results, plane with the grain. Continually sight the edge against a steel ruler and the mating piece until you see no daylight in the joint.

4. Glue the panels. Apply glue sparingly—just a thin bead along the edge of one piece. There should be no squeeze-out when you clamp the pieces together. If you do use too much glue, touch the edge with the excess on a dust-free surface to remove the extra glue. Be sure the faces are flush and then clamp the pieces together with light pressure. After an hour, gently scrape off any excess glue from the face. If the joint is not perfect, open it with a hot iron and start again. The next day, when the glue has set, scrape away excess from the underside and sand the face with a random-orbit sander and P150-grit paper.

Bending Tips

Cut the wood you are bending at least 1" (25mm) longer than needed in case you misjudge the curve position and run off the end.

Use the bending strap to heat and bend the wood initially. When the wood softens and the curve begins to take shape, remove the strap so you can refine the curve.

Use a light, steady touch. Too much pressure on tight curves will crease or crack the wood.

Fortunately, you can repair small cracks and splits with cyanoacrylate adhesive.

Avoid scorching the wood. It takes an age to sand out the scorch marks.

Hold the wood square to the bending iron; if you don't, you will introduce a twist.

Use a spray bottle or a damp towel between the iron and the wood when you need an extra shot of steam.

BEND THE SIDE PIECES

If you have never bent wood over a hot pipe or bending iron, practice bending several pieces of scrap wood until you become familiar with the process. It will take the pressure off when you go to bend the good wood for your ukulele.

You can also use the practice pieces to work through other building steps, like adding a section of lining and a top surface or flush trimming and rabbeting with a router. This way, you can hone your skills and see how your chosen wood will perform during each process. And it will save you a lot of angst.

Prepare the jig and bending iron

5. Make a body jig. A jig is the form that will help you shape the sides of your ukulele. It is used throughout the construction process to keep the body properly shaped. Trace the ukulele body shape directly on to a piece of ¾" (19mm) medium-density fiberboard or plywood and draw a centerline down the length of the profile. Cut out half the shape with a band saw or jigsaw. Sand the edge smooth and be sure the curves are smooth and fair. Trace the cut-out shape on another piece of medium-density fiberboard or plywood, saw it so it is slightly oversized, and nail it to the first piece. Use a router with a flush-trim bit to smooth the curves on the second piece. Repeat until you have two identical jigs that are the depth of your ukulele.

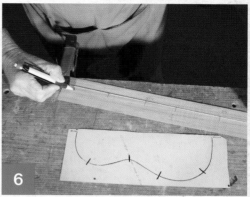

6. Make a bending pattern. Using the body jig as a guide, take a permanent marker and trace the ukulele shape onto a waterproof surface (a piece of medium-density fiberboard covered with packing tape works). You will use this as a reference when you bend the wood for the sides. Lay a piece of string along the bending-pattern line. Mark the start, midpoint, and end of each curve on the string. Use a pencil to transfer the marks to the wood you will use for the sides. These markings will allow you to know where to begin and end each bend.

7. Make (or buy) a bending iron. A heated bending iron warms dampened wood to produce steam, which helps shape the wood into a curve. You can buy an electric iron, or, following the plan on page 64, you can make an excellent one yourself from a length of 1½" (38mm) galvanized water pipe and heat it with a propane torch. A blacksmith or machinist can make the iron if you aren't familiar with metalworking. To make your own bending iron, take a 24" (610mm) length of pipe and smooth the outside with emery cloth. Weld a 4" (102mm) piece of ⅜" (10mm) steel rod along the top at the torch end and a bracket on the bottom so the pipe can be firmly held in a vise. The thin rod is for bending tight curves. Weld another rod at the torch end, which is also welded to a smaller-diameter pipe or elbow for the torch nozzle, so the flame is directed into the bending pipe. Make a bending strap from a thin sheet of galvanized steel roof flashing. It supports the wood against the bending iron and helps you create smooth curves. The strap also helps distribute the steam through the wood.

Hot Pipe Safety

Remove any flammable liquids from the workshop. Sweep debris off the bench. Wear leather gloves to protect your hands from scalding by steam. Most importantly, always be aware that the exhaust end of the gas-bending pipe can be hot. Be sure everything is cool to the touch before you dismantle the bending iron.

FOLLOW THIS PLAN TO MAKE YOUR OWN BENDING IRON.

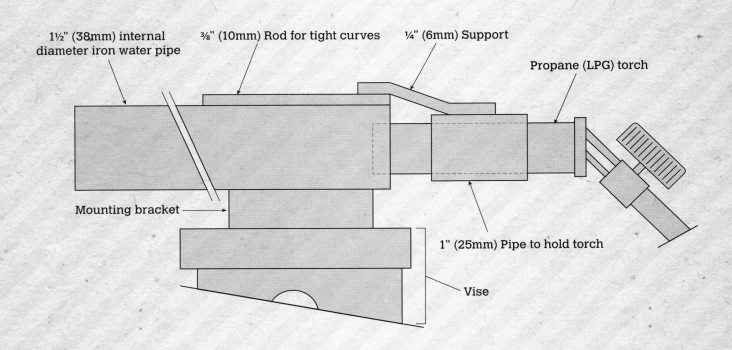

1½" (38mm) internal diameter iron water pipe

⅜" (10mm) Rod for tight curves

¼" (6mm) Support

Propane (LPG) torch

Mounting bracket

1" (25mm) Pipe to hold torch

Vise

This shop-made bending iron is an inexpensive alternative to purchasing a commercial iron.

If you don't fancy working with an open flame, you can buy an electric bending iron like this. It's just as effective as a pipe heated with a torch, but more expensive.

Bend the sides

8. Practice. It takes practice to learn to bend wood, so spend some time working with scrap wood to determine the optimum temperature of the iron and moisture content of the wood. Once you get some practice, hot-pipe bending will seem so easy. Given the right conditions, most woods will bend readily. However, mahogany and all types of figured wood are more difficult to bend and need to be treated differently. Because the grain in figured wood runs in all directions and is sometimes stacked like the pile on a carpet, it is very fragile. Soaking this wood will cause the grain to separate and lead to broken curves. To bend figured wood, fold it in a piece of heavy brown paper that has been sprayed with water. Iron both sides on a flat surface to generate steam. Leave the wood wrapped in the paper and sandwich it between a wet rag and the bending strap as you begin to move it over the hot pipe. Give the paper a light spray of water if it seems to be drying too quickly.

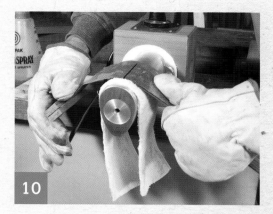

9. Heat the iron and achieve a consistent temperature. Heat the iron to between 350° and 400°F (177°–204°C) at the midpoint; use a surface thermometer to check the temperature. Lower the flame so the temperature remains constant throughout the process. The surface temperature of the iron will vary along its length; so if you do not have a thermometer, experiment with practice wood to find a constant working temperature. You can control the amount of heat transferred to the wood by the position of the wood along the pipe, the moisture content of the wood, the time it spends in contact with the pipe, and the use of a heat shield like damp fabric or heavy brown paper; more reasons to practice.

10. Make the first bend. Soak straight-grained wood for up to ten minutes. Wet a strip of toweling, wring it out, and drape it over the bending iron. Place the wood on the fabric with the bending strap on the top. Hold the towel, wood, and strap together. Heat the section you want to curve by rolling and sliding the wood over the iron. Steam from the towel will relax the wood fibers, allowing it to bend. Bend the center curve, at the waist, first. When you begin a bend, use the bending strap to hold the steam in the wood, heat the side, and start the bend. Remove the strap and slide the wet fabric along under the wood to continually generate steam and finish the bend.

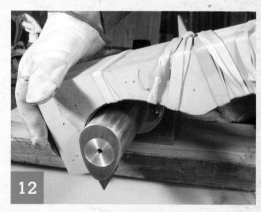

11. Make the second and third bends. Once you are satisfied with the curve at the waist, flip the wood over and make the bends at either end of the side piece.

12. Check against the jig. Check the curves you create against the body jig. Use a spray bottle to moisten the wood if necessary and refine the curve. When the curve matches the body jig, dry the wood over the iron; wet wood can cup if it is allowed to dry in the jig.

13. Dry and re-bend as needed. After you have dried the wood, use plenty of rubber bands to clamp the finished side into the body jig. Leave it overnight and check it the next morning for spring back—where the released side does not fit the mold. Re-bend if necessary, using a light spray of water, with or without a wet rag. Heat the side piece while it is still in the mold, which will trap the generated steam. Once you have finished, reattach it to the mold with rubber bands.

ASSEMBLE THE BODY

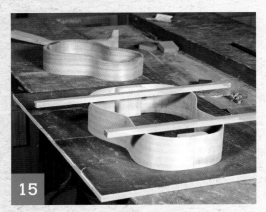

14. Square up the sides and glue them together. Fit the bent sides into the body jig. Orient them with the top edges down on a flat surface. Trim the protruding ends flush with each end of the jig so you will have a tight, square joint when you clamp the halves of the jig together. If the ends don't come together tightly, use a rubber band as a shim between the wood and the jig. Glue and clamp the heel and neck blocks in place. If you plan to attach the neck with a mortise-and-tenon joint (the alternative is a butt joint; see page 52, step 18), cut the mortise in the neck block before gluing it in position.

15. Sand the edges. When the glue has set, sand the sides square and flush with the end blocks. When sanding, keep the edges square and sharp with no warp or wind over the gluing surface. You can use a stationary belt sander at first, but be aware that it can be quite aggressive. Finish sanding by hand, using a large sheet of 100-grit paper glued to a flat board so you can sand all the edges at once. Use winding sticks (see photo) to check for warping.

16. Make (or buy) the lining. The lining is a thin strip added along the top edge of the sides to increase the gluing surface on the joint between the sides, top, and bottom. You can buy lining already made, or make your own by cutting lengths of stock with a fine-tooth blade on a table saw or band saw. Take the dimensions from the plan on page 58. Cut the kerf slots on a band saw, using a jig like the one shown in the photo. The slot in the jig, where the blade sits, serves as a stop block to control the depth of the kerfs. Put a pencil mark on the jig ¾₁₆" (5mm) from one side of the blade to gauge the spacing between cuts.

17. Attach the lining. Place the body back in the jig so the top edge protrudes ½" (13mm). Clamp the halves of the jig together to hold the body firmly in place. Moisten the lining to make it more flexible and clamp it in place with clothespins. When the wood has dried, glue it in place, again using clothespin clamps. Sand the lining flush with the side. Repeat these two steps to attach the lining to the bottom edge.

18. Shape the soundboard. Place the soundboard face down on a smooth surface. Place the body over it and align the body end joints with the center of the soundboard. (If you have made the soundboard from a single piece, draw a center line along the grain and work from that.) Trace the inside and outside of the body. Cut out the soundboard on the band saw, making it oversized to allow for any tearout. Mark the position of the braces and sound hole, following the plan on page 57.

19. Cut and insert the braces. The braces need to be light so the soundboard can vibrate, yet strong enough to keep the top flat when under stress. Use wood with a tight, even grain and cut the braces so the grain runs parallel to the thickest side. Refine their shape on a belt sander, glue them in place, and clamp them with weights.

20. Secure the soundboard for gluing. To keep the soundboard from slipping out of place when it is clamped down, use two fine wire brads to index it to the body. Drive a brad in each end block and snip them almost flush with the wood with wire cutters. Lay the body in position on the soundboard and tap each end block lightly to push the brads into the top.

21. Glue and clamp the soundboard. Dry-clamp the soundboard in position with rubber bands or weights and check for gaps in the joint. Sand or scrape any high spots until the soundboard fits evenly. When everything looks spot on, glue the body and soundboard together.

22. Flush-trim the top. Now, go over the body with a router to bring the soundboard flush with the sides. Later, you will repeat this step to cut a small rabbet in the joint to house decorative binding. Do this work on a router table if you have one. If you are using a handheld router, clamp the body into the body jig and the jig to the bench. Make a test run on your practice body piece. Follow the sequence of cuts shown in the drawing to minimize tearout. There will be a tendency for the router to skip, so keep it firmly under control. Take several small passes, working down to the final cut. Finish the trimming and rabbeting with a climb cut—moving the router around the edge against the rotation of the bit. To help reduce tearout when routing long-grained brittle woods like western red cedar, acacia, or spruce, put clear packaging tape over the top surface. Reduce the tack of the tape by first pressing it onto a cotton t-shirt. When removing the tape, pull gently along the grain and toward the cut edge. You can also use a hair dryer to soften the tape adhesive. Remove any adhesive residue with acetone.

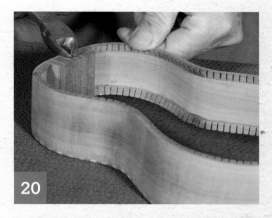

20

21

22 Cut 1–4 with cutter direction
Cut 5 finish-cut all around opposite direction

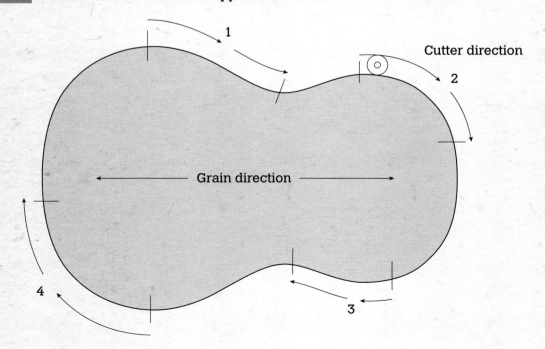

1

Cutter direction

2

Grain direction

3

4

MAKE THE BINDING

The binding around the edges of a ukulele not only looks good, but also protects the edges and strengthens the joints. You can buy ready-made plastic or wood binding in a wide range of sizes, colors, and patterns, but it's very easy to make your own.

Wood binding can be easily sawn on a table saw and sized with a drill-press sander. Try laminating two different-colored strips of wood to make the binding, or go all out and give your ukulele the traditional look of a vintage instrument with wood rope binding.

23. Rip the stock and glue up billets. Select two or three contrasting woods and saw 1" (25mm)-wide strips to finish at 0.10" (2.5mm) thick on your drum or drill-press sander. For a 1" by 0.10" (25 x 2.5mm) strip, a total length of 120" (3048mm) for all the woods will give you plenty of material. Cut the strips into 6" (152mm) lengths and arrange them in an angled stack, using a bevel gauge set at 40 degrees, alternating the woods. Glue the strips, rubbing them together to distribute the glue. Do not use clamps, which tend to push the strips out of alignment.

24. Cut the billets to make strips of binding. When the glue has set, sand off the staggered ends with a belt sander and square the edges on the band saw. Hold the stack at 40 degrees to the band saw blade and resaw the stack in half along its length. Stack and glue the halves together. When dry, repeat the resawing and gluing to produce a stack about 6" (152mm) long. Sand each edge flat and saw the stack into ⅛" (3mm)-thick slabs.

Drill-Press Sander

This is very useful sander for finishing small pieces of wood. It is a sanding drum fitted to a drill-press chuck. By adding a simple fence, you can make it a handy thickness sander.

You can buy a sleeved drum or turn one from a block 4" x 3" (102 x 76mm) square. Drill a ⅜" (10mm) hole in the center of one end and secure a drill bit or length of steel rod in the hole with epoxy. Chuck this shaft in the lathe, position the tailpiece, and then turn a cylinder. Saw a ¼" (6mm)-deep slot along the length of the cylinder.

Tuck sandpaper into the slot, wind it around the drum, and cut it just short of the slot. Secure the loose end with contact cement.

When the drum is fitted to the drill press, house the bottom in a hole cut into a piece of medium-density fiberboard that is securely clamped to the drill-press table and bring the table up to the sander.

For thickness sanding, clamp a fence to the drill-press table. Adjust the fence by loosening one clamp and lightly tapping the fence into position.

25. Thickness-sand the binding. Thickness-sand both sides of the slabs to bring them to a final thickness of 0.10" (2.5mm). Saw the slabs into strips and sand the strips to 0.10" (2.5mm) on the drill press sander, supporting the strips in a rabbet cut into a flat piece of wood.

26. Rout a rabbet. Use a bearing-guided rabbet bit to give a cut of about 0.06" x 0.012" (1.5 x 0.3mm) in the body for single bindings and 0.1" x 0.1" (2.5 x 2.5mm) for laminated and rope bindings. Luthier suppliers sell specialized router bits, but, depending on the size of the binding you want to use, you may be able to juggle the bearings on a standard-sized bit to do the job. To avoid tearout, follow the same sequence of cuts as for flush-trimming. See the drawing on page 67.

27. Fit the binding. Bend the binding to fit the rabbet. Plastic binding will bend to shape with a little heat from a hair dryer or heat gun, and you can bend one-piece wood strip binding on a bending iron. Rope binding is more fragile. Use gentle heat to bend it: Place the binding between two pieces of moist brown paper and iron both sides with a gentle setting on the household iron so as not to melt the glue joints. Do a test fit with a sample glued to your practice body, to find out how well the binding conforms to tight curves. When your test sample has dried, measure the fit to the rabbet and resize the rest of your binding stock if necessary to ensure a minimum of scraping and sanding back to size.

28. Glue the binding. Apply glue to the rabbet and work the rope binding into place, taping it down as you go. With one-piece binding, dry fit, tape it in place, and leave it for a day or two. When you are ready to glue the binding in place, first be sure you have plenty of rubber bands and tape on hand to use as clamps. I use Weldon #16 for plastic binding and wood glue like Titebond for wood bindings. Both have a long open time, meaning they give you plenty of time to fit the binding before they begin to set. Apply the glue to the rabbet, smooth it out with your finger, and fit the binding. Lift a small part of the binding to check your glue coverage. When the glue has dried, remove the tape and rubber bands and check the binding for gaps; close them by heating the top and then the side of the binding with an iron. This will soften the adhesive so you can push the binding into place with a cork block and hold it in place while the glue sets again.

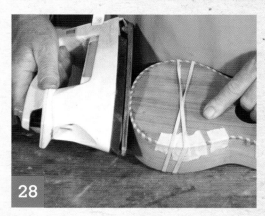

29. Sand the binding flush. Allow the glue to set fully. If you are using wood binding, wait for a couple of days to let it dry out and shrink. Scrape and sand every trace of glue from the surface and sand the binding flush. With rope binding, also round over the edge to give it a "laid rope" appearance. Check for glue residue by wiping the wood surface with paint thinner or naphtha. Use a cabinet scraper to pare plastic bindings flush to the body; sand with 800-grit paper to remove any scratches.

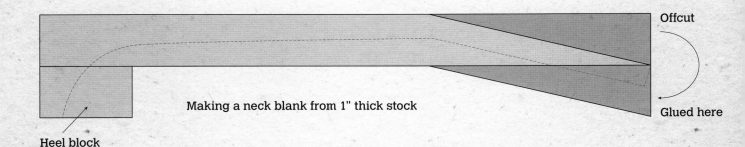

Offcut

Glued here

Making a neck blank from 1" thick stock

Heel block

30

31

CONSTRUCT THE NECK

30. Cut the neck blank. You can make a thick neck blank from thin stock. Say you have wood boards that are 1" (25mm) thick, but you need a blank of twice that thickness. As the drawing shows, take a tapered offcut and glue it to the underside of the head to make it the correct thickness. Glue a block at the other end at the neck joint. For maximum strength, use a piece of close-grained wood for the neck, or laminate thin stock to build up a blank.

31. Saw the head angle and add reference lines. Make a tapering jig for the table saw using the plan on page 71. Take two boards that are about 24" x 4" x ¾" (610 x 102 x 19mm). Hinge them together at one end and fit a stop block on the end of one board. On the neck blank, mark the position of the nut; that determines where the head angle will begin. Find the head angle from the plan and draw it on the side of the neck blank. Use double-sided tape to hold the neck blank on the tapering jig; position the head against the stop block and the nut mark to the rear and facing the blade. Open the hinge until the head angle line is parallel with the other leg of the jig. Screw a brace across the legs to hold them in position. Set the table saw fence and saw the head angle. Sand or plane the top face of the head. Draw a centerline on the top face of the neck blank and square off a line at the nut position. Transfer all measurements from the plan using these two reference lines. Measure the distance from the nut to the body joint. Mark out the fingerboard detail from the centerline.

32. Draw the head shape. Make a medium-density fiberboard template of half the head shape. Drill two ⅛" (3mm) holes at the tuner positions. Align the template with the centerline and nut position lines on the neck blank. Trace the outline and mark the tuner positions with a sharpened ⅛" (3mm) nail through the template holes. Flip the template and repeat for the other side.

33. Make the neck joint. The easiest way to attach the neck to the body is with a simple butt joint, with the neck glued in place and held with screws through the neck block. I recommend the butt joint for beginners, because you can sand the neck to adjust its angle up and down and from side to side, assuring perfect fit and alignment. Cut the joint square before you go on to shape the blank.

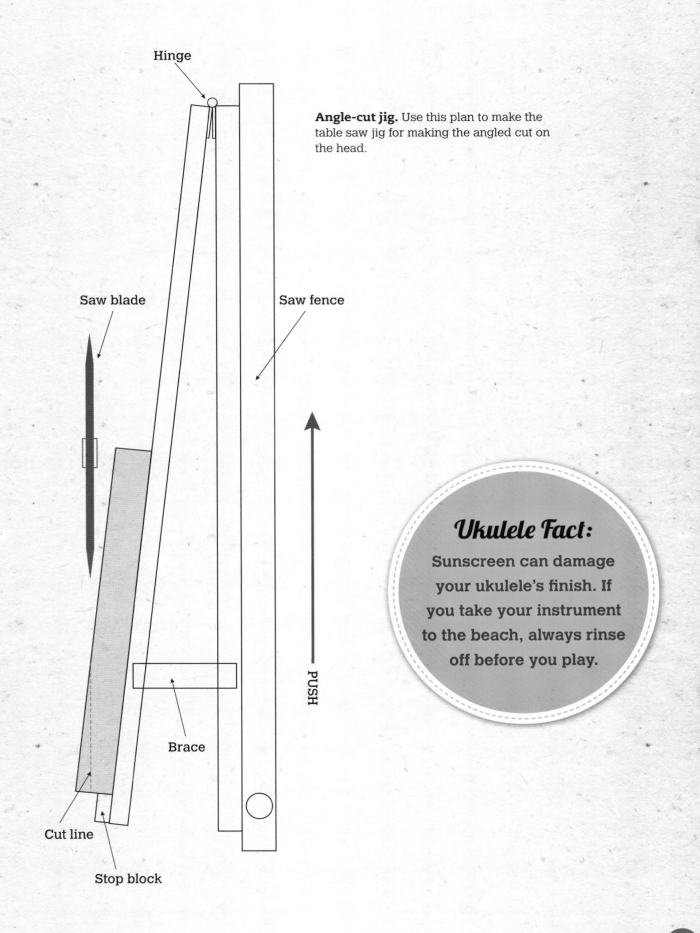

Hinge

Angle-cut jig. Use this plan to make the table saw jig for making the angled cut on the head.

Saw blade

Saw fence

PUSH

Brace

Cut line

Stop block

Ukulele Fact:

Sunscreen can damage your ukulele's finish. If you take your instrument to the beach, always rinse off before you play.

34. Rough out the neck. Trace the neck profile onto the side of the neck blank. (Also trace the profile onto a piece of medium-density fiberboard or plywood and cut it out to use as a guide for the final shaping.) For the first cut, use a ½" (13mm) resaw blade. Cut the underside of the head to make it the proper thickness. Change to a narrow blade with 4 to 6 teeth per inch (25mm) and finish cutting the profile. Next, cut the head shape. You will need to stack some blocks on the band saw table to support the head so you can make right-angle cuts. You can square up the sides by finish-sanding on the drill-press sander. Cut the side profiles with the band saw table set at an angle. The plan shows the taper of the V-shape on each side of the neck where it meets the body. Set the band saw table to that angle. With the neck blank right side up, carefully saw both sides.

35. Refine the neck shape with a rasp. This step is quite easy. It is great to see and feel the finished neck emerge from the sawn blank. Use the extra profile you cut earlier to sight your work as you shape. To hold the neck blank as you shape it, make a jig from 2x4 (38 x 89mm) lumber, shaped to match the angle of the top of the blank. Before clamping the neck blank into the jig, carefully sand the top edge of the blank almost down to the line marking the fingerboard position and run a good thick chalk line along that edge. Then, place the jig in a vise and clamp the neck to it. Get the feel of your rasps by shaping a neck from scrap. Experiment with the cutting technique and tools in a variety of lighting angles to highlight irregularities. Run your hands over your work and you will develop a feel for both symmetry and defects in the emerging shape. For the preliminary shaping, hold the rasp at 45 degrees to the grain; this will give you a controlled aggressive cut. The most common mistake in shaping the neck is to leave too much wood. Be brave and shape close to the plan profile. When you begin to remove the chalk, you are done. Check the profile and stop.

36. Finish with sandpaper. Continue shaping the neck with a 4" (102mm) rubber sanding disc mounted on a drill press. Use a thin flexible 4" (102mm) backing disc with 80-, 100-, and 150-grit paper. As you sand through the grits, be sure to remove any scratch patterns from the previous grit and be careful not to cut into inside curves with the edge of the paper. All that remains is to sand the tight inside curves and give the neck a smooth, scratch-free finish. Use a fine detail sander and finish by hand with 220-grit paper. Position a reading lamp at a low angle and ruthlessly check for scratches or uneven surfaces. Go back and sand them out.

MAKE THE FINGERBOARD

The fingerboard gets a lot of wear, so it needs to be made from durable wood. Ebony and rosewood are commonly used for guitar fingerboards, but any hardwood will work for a ukulele because the strings are light. Work with a rectangular blank when cutting slots for the frets and drilling holes for the marker dots. Then cut the fingerboard to suit the neck shape.

37. Locate the fret positions. The ukulele's scale length determines the fret positions on the fingerboard. The scale length is the distance from the front edge of the nut to where the strings contact the bridge. The twelfth fret is positioned at exactly half the scale distance. If you have designed your own ukulele, determine its scale length and go to the online fret calculator at *www.stewmac.com/fretcalc.html* for tables of fret measurements. Do not take fret positions directly from a drawing, but work from the table and measure each fret position from the guideline you drew on the neck for the nut position. This way, you avoid the possibility of a cumulative error if you measure from fret to fret. If you're following the plan in this book, use it to determine the scale length (see page 74). Measure and mark each fret position by making a small knife cut at the edge of the blank. Make a simple miter box, as shown in the photo, and cut the fret slots with a fret saw or a Japanese backsaw with a .023" (0.6mm) kerf. Clamp a ruler to the saw to set the cutting depth.

38. Add the marker dots. The marker dots are a guide to the fret positions when playing. Measure the position of the marker dots relative to the position of the frets. Clamp a fence to the drill press table so the holes for the dots are centered on the fingerboard. Set the depth stop to suit the inlay. To avoid tearout, use a brad-point bit. You can choose from a wide range of pre-cut inlays or create your own dots by filling the holes with colored epoxy. Mix the epoxy carefully to avoid air bubbles and color it with lampblack. Blow any sawdust from the holes and carefully overfill them; the epoxy will shrink a little as it sets. Sand the dots flush with the wood and polish with fine-grade paper.

39. Shape the fingerboard. Nail two fine wire brads to the neck and cut them almost flush with the surface with wire cutters, leaving them with a nice, sharp point. Center the fingerboard over the neck and clamp it lightly to press it down on the brads. Trace the shape of the neck on the back of the fingerboard, remove it, and cut it to size. Reattach the fingerboard and sand it flush with the neck. Remove it again so you can fit the frets.

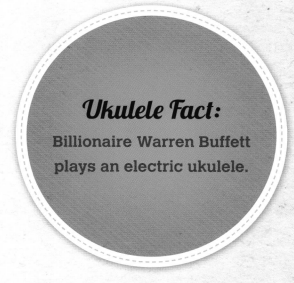

Ukulele Fact:
Billionaire Warren Buffett plays an electric ukulele.

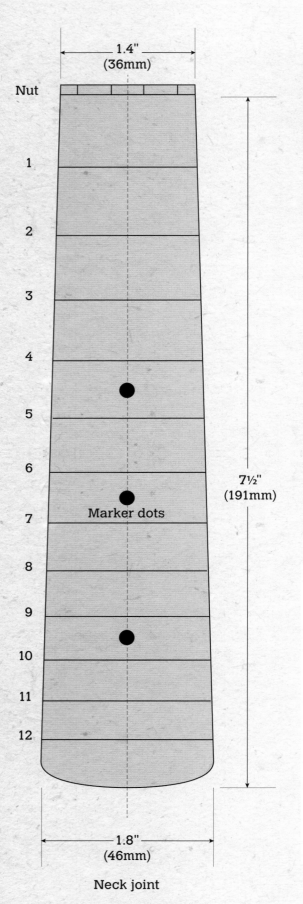

Nut

1.4"
(36mm)

Nut

1

2

3

4

5

6

7

Marker dots

8

9

10

11

12

7½"
(191mm)

1.8"
(46mm)

Neck joint

40

40. Fit and finish the frets. Cut the fretwire so it is slightly oversized. You can press the fretwire into the slots with a drill press and a block of wood, or use a plastic-faced mallet and a block of wood. Seat the fretwire with one or two taps; too much hammering will result in a fret that is too low or poorly seated. Check that the fret is vertical. Sometimes when cutting fret slots, you may rock the saw and cut too deeply at one end of the cut, leaving a small gap visible under the fretwire on the side of the fingerboard. Put a small drop of cyanoacrylate adhesive in the hole and sand the edge with fine paper until sawdust fills the hole. If you cut a slot slightly wide or have a loose fret, carefully remove the fretwire, place packaging tape over the slot, and cut through the tape into the slot. Spread a drop of cyanoacrylate along the slot and re-seat the fret. Use the drill press drum sander to bring the ends of the fretwire flush with the sides of the fingerboard. Cover the edges of the fingerboard with heavy masking tape or binding tape to protect the wood and use a fine flat file to file through the tape and round over the fret ends at a 45-degree angle. Then use a three-corner file to remove sharp edges. Finish the ends with emery paper. Set the fingerboard aside until you have attached the neck to the body.

13.97" (355mm) Fret Scale

Fret number	Distance from nut	Distance between frets
1	0.784" (20mm)	Nut–fret 1: 0.784" (20mm)
2	1.524" (39mm)	Fret 1–2: 0.740" (19mm)
3	2.223" (56mm)	Fret 2–3: 0.699" (18mm)
4	2.882" (73mm)	Fret 3–4: 0.659" (17mm)
5	3.504" (89mm)	Fret 4–5: 0.622" (16mm)
6	4.092" (104mm)	Fret 5–6: 0.588" (15mm)
7	4.646" (118mm)	Fret 6–7: 0.544" (14mm)
8	5.169" (131mm)	Fret 7–8: 0.523" (13mm)
9	5.663" (144mm)	Fret 8–9: 0.494" (13mm)
10	6.130" (156mm)	Fret 9–10: 0.467" (12mm)
11	6.570" (167mm)	Fret 10–11: 0.440" (11mm)
12	6.985" (177mm)	Fret 11–12: 0.415" (11mm)

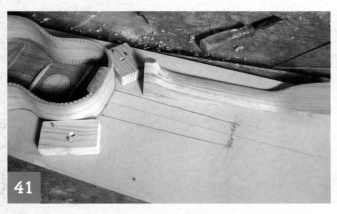

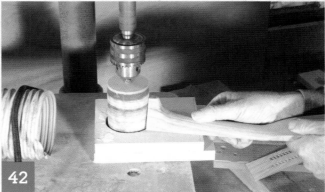

41. Align the parts. Trace the outline of the body onto a piece of medium-density fiberboard and attach blocks around the perimeter to hold the body firmly in place. Remove the body and draw a centerline through the ukulele shape, extending it well past the top. Align everything using this line and you will not go wrong. Replace the body and put the neck in position, centering it on the centerline. Trace the sides of the neck onto the medium-density fiberboard. Remove the neck and make sure the guidelines you drew are equidistant from the centerline. Attach a holding block along each side.

42. Fit the joint. Position the neck against the body and check the fit of the joint. If you made a butt joint, first shape the end on a spindle or drill press sander so that it conforms to the shape of the body.

Ukulele Fact:

The ukulele made an appearance in the movie *50 First Dates* and on the hit TV show *Scrubs*.

Cutting a Mortise-and-Tenon Joint

Cut the mortise in the neck block before assembling the body sides. Once the sides are bent and glued, flush-trim them to the joint. Cut the tenon on the neck blank before it is shaped. Use a tall auxiliary fence, like the one shown in photo 1, or a tenoning jig, to make the first cuts defining the tenon on the neck. Support the stock with a table saw miter gauge or a crosscut sled to cut the tenon shoulders. To avoid kickback, keep the miter fence away from the cut, as shown in photo 2.

Define the tenon.

Cut the shoulders.

43

44

FIT THE NECK TO THE BODY

43. Attach the neck and fingerboard. I find epoxy ideal for attaching the neck. It has a long open time, good gap-filling qualities, and does not show "milky" under a lacquer finish. (If you find a visible gap in the neck joint, make a filler from epoxy and fine sanding dust.) Glue the neck in position and check that the body and neck are flat on the medium-density fiberboard. Push the neck firmly against the body. Clamp it lightly in position with a large rubber band, as shown in the photo. Clean up any squeeze-out with a sharpened paint scraper and wipe the joint with a cotton swab barely dampened with acetone. A butt joint can be further strengthened with wood screws. After the glue has set, drill and countersink two pilot holes through the neck block into the neck and drive in the screws. Cover the screw heads with a thin piece of wood glued to the neck block. Clean up the top of the joint and glue the fingerboard in place with wood glue. Clamp it with rubber bands. Some very dry fingerboards will absorb moisture from the glue and bow away from the neck, leaving a fine gap at each edge. To counter this tendency, spray water on the top surface of the fingerboard before gluing.

PHOTO BY BENGT NYMAN.

Bill Tapia

Ukulele legend Bill Tapia, who celebrated his 103rd birthday in 2011, has been playing the ukulele since he was a young boy. Born in Honolulu, Tapia used to serenade tourists visiting the Hawaiian Islands. From that point on, Tapia's popularity as a ukulele and guitar player grew. He played at the opening of the Royal Hawaiian Hotel and formed his own group, Tappy's Island Swingers. Tapia loves jazz music, and moved to the mainland United States for an opportunity to play. His jazz career was based around the guitar, but in 2001 and 2002, Tapia returned to the music scene as a ukulele performer.

TUNE THE SOUNDBOARD

There is a lot of mystique and many different ideas on how to tune a soundboard, but don't worry too much. Tuning is only one part of making a great-sounding ukulele. The instrument has a relatively small soundboard, which makes it stronger and therefore gives you a greater margin for error.

44. Tap, listen, and trim. The secret of tuning is to hold the ukulele by the neck and tap the soundboard with your knuckle, listen to the sound, then shave the bracing evenly and in small increments. Work with a very sharp chisel so you can easily pare thin shavings from the bracing. Thinning the braces gives the soundboard a brighter tone. Alternate this tap-tuning between the top and the bottom section of the soundboard. The narrow top end will have a higher tap tone; it handles the treble end of the instrument's range. The wider bottom end will have a bright, but mellower, tone. Initially, the tap tone will be quite clunky. When you tap and trim, you will delight in hearing the tone sweeten up and become brighter. Stop paring when you hear that change in tone.

INSTALL THE BACK

45. Sand the open back body. It will be flat or arched, depending on the plan. Check it with winding sticks to ensure the sides are of an even height, as you did when shaping the top.

46. Cut out the back and add braces. Mark and cut the back, making it slightly oversized. Mark out the brace positions. Cut and shape the braces, then glue them in place as you did with the braces for the soundboard.

47. Tap and tune. Give the back a tap while holding it lightly at the edge between your thumb and forefinger. Pare down the braces until you are satisfied with the tone. If you want to add an integrated pickup to amplify the sound electrically (see page 78), install it now.

48. Glue the back in place. Put locating brads into the end blocks of the body. Fit the back, pressing it down into the brads. Place the ukulele in the medium-density fiberboard jig you used to attach the neck. Make sure the neck is flat on the board and then glue and clamp the back in position with weights.

Fun Facts about Hawaii

- In 2009, Hawaii celebrated its fiftieth year as a state.

- Geographically, Hawaii is one of the most remote places on earth, about 2,400 miles (3862km) from the western United States, close to 4,000 miles (6437km) from Japan, and almost 5,000 miles (8047km) from China.

- The state is divided into four counties: Honolulu, Kauai, Maui, and Hawaii.

- Hawaii is the only state in the union to grow coffee, and produces more than 300,000 tons (272,155 metric tons) of pineapples a year.

- If you're planning a vacation, you should know Hawaii has its own time zone and does not use daylight saving time. This means Pacific Time on the mainland is two hours ahead of Hawaii in the summer, and three hours ahead in the winter.

Ukulele Tip:

If you live in a dry or cold area, use a humidifier to protect your ukulele.

Add a Pickup

Amplified music is becoming more popular with part-time players who often participate in open mic sessions, community concerts, and church groups. A pickup allows the ukulele's notes to be amplified through a sound system.

There are several ways to amplify the ukulele's sound:

Microphone. The simplest way to create more sound is to play in front of a microphone that will pick up both your voice and instrument. This is a good system for ukulele groups but can be prone to feedback, that shattering howl heard when the microphone picks up sound from the speakers and feeds it back through the system.

Piezo pickup

Under-saddle pickup

Soundboard transducer. This is a simple piezo pickup attached to the outside or inside of the soundboard, transmitting the sound by wire to the amplifier. This type of pickup can be mounted with a suction cup or Blu-Tack temporary adhesive and moved from instrument to instrument. A transducer can be a bit clunky or woody sounding and will pick up quite a bit of handling noise from the instrument body. It's best to mount a transducer under or near the bridge.

Under-saddle pickup. This is a strip-type piezo pickup that fits permanently in the bridge under the saddle. A small hole drilled through the soundboard carries a wire attached to a socket either on the side of the body or in the endpin where the strap is attached to the body. An under-saddle pickup is less prone to feedback than the other types.

CONSTRUCT THE BRIDGE

49. Shape the bridge. When making the bridge, it is safer to work with a piece of wood long enough for you to handle safely around a table saw and router table. Joint and plane a length of wood to the proper width and thickness and round over the long edges with a router. To avoid injury when shaping a small, thin piece like this, use featherboards to guide the stock as it passes across the router bit. Following the plan on page 58, cut a ³⁄₃₂" (2.5mm) slot on a router table to house a bone saddle. A ³⁄₃₂" (2.5mm) router bit is a specialized size available from a luthier supplier. Rout carefully to ensure the slot is a uniform depth, for maximum contact with the saddle or pickup.

49

50. Mark and cut the string slots. Following the measurements on the plan, clamp the bottom of the bridge to a piece of scrap wood and drill a hole at each slot, centering the drill bit on the seam between the bridge and the scrap piece. Remove the scrap and you have half-circle recesses for the knots. Use a coping saw to cut four slots in the rear edge to take the strings.

50

INSTALL THE NUT

Nuts and saddles are traditionally made from bone; ready-made plastic and composite alternatives are also available.

51. Shape the bone. If you decide on a bone nut and saddle and wish to make your own, use a thighbone from a cow. Get a fresh one from the butcher, cut off the ends, and clean out the marrow. Boil the bone for ten minutes and hang it to dry for a few days. (I once left a bone on the bench, the dog buried it somewhere in the yard, and I haven't seen it since.) You can easily cut bone using a band saw, but be sure to hold it firmly when sawing so it does not twist, jam, and break the blade. Cut out the nut blank and shape it with a file or sandpaper stuck to a flat surface. Begin shaping with 100-grit sandpaper, working up to 220-grit. Make sure the bottom edge is square so the nut will butt tight against the fingerboard. Round over the back and sides. The nut should protrude 0.075" (2mm) above the fret height.

52. Mark the string slots and glue down the nut. Sandwich the blank between two pieces of medium-density fiberboard and clamp everything in a vise. Mark the slot positions. Use a fretsaw to cut shallow starting slots and rub out the pencil marks. Then, step back and see if the slots look right. If not, you can make adjustments when you cut the slots deeper, once the nut is in place. Glue the nut in position with epoxy. The final string slots need to match the diameter of the string, with a whisker of clearance to allow the string to move without catching in the slot. If the slot is too wide, the string will vibrate in the gap and make an annoying buzz. If you cut a slot too deep, the string will buzz against the first fret; too shallow, and the string will be too high and hard to play. Proceed carefully. If you do make a slot too deep, fill it with cyanoacrylate adhesive and baking soda, allow it to set, then re-cut the slot.

Ukulele Fact:
In 2006, Samuel Kamaka's ukulele company celebrated 90 years in business.

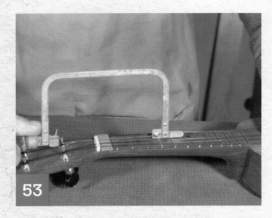

53. **Finish cutting the string slots.** Use round-bottom luthier slot files or a coping saw blade to match the string diameter. (If you use a saw blade, gently soften the bottom of the slot with a piece of fine folded emery cloth.) Make some trial cuts in scrap bone. The ideal string height is 0.03" (0.8mm) above the first fret. Make a gauge so you can cut the slots in the nut to that dimension and avoid damaging the head or fingerboard. Assume that the fret height is 0.037" (0.9mm). That means the bottom of the slot should be 0.067" (2mm) above the fingerboard. Stack strips of plastic or cardboard to a thickness of 0.067" (2mm). Check the thickness with a Vernier caliper. Position the gauge on the fingerboard next to the nut and finish cutting the slots down to the gauge. This should result in a good playing action. However, you can fine-tune the depth of the slots if necessary. Lubricate the slots with a graphite pencil.

ATTACH THE BRIDGE

If this is your first attempt at building an instrument, you may find that the neck is marginally out of line with the body because the body may be slightly misshapen or the neck not truly centered. In that case, if you attach the bridge in the center of the soundboard, the strings will be out of line with the fingerboard and sound hole. Some makers like to intentionally offset the strings slightly to the right to compensate for the left hand fretting action. It is up to you to decide how you want to align the strings on your instrument.

54. **Check the bridge alignment.** Before gluing down the bridge, check to be sure the strings will be properly aligned. Measure the scale length from the front edge of the nut and draw a line on the body at a right angle to the centerline at that point. This line marks where the strings contact the bridge saddle. Attach a length of yarn to an outside slot of the bridge, run it over the nut, down behind the head, back over the nut, and down to the other outside slot on the bridge. The yarn must be long enough for you to hold the bridge in position. Weight the yarn behind the head to keep it taut. Place the yarn in the appropriate nut slot and move the bridge from side to side until it is aligned with the fingerboard and the sound hole. Mark the bridge position with tape and double check the scale length.

55. **Glue the bridge to the soundboard.** Glue the bridge to the soundboard at the position you marked and clamp it lightly. Epoxy is good for this, because any traces of the adhesive will not show under the final finish. Congratulations! This is the final step in assembling your ukulele. All that remains is to apply the finish, fit the strings, and adjust the bridge height.

FINISH THE WOOD

So far you have put a lot of care and effort into building your ukulele. Make sure that you maintain this high standard of workmanship throughout the finishing process. It's natural to want to rush, now that you're so close to completing the instrument. Resist this urge: take a walk, read a book, have dinner with friends.

56. **Clean surfaces and remove defects.** Sand and scrape off all traces of glue from the surface of the wood. Check for glue residue and fine scratches by wiping the surface with thinners. Always sand and scrape with the grain. This means you scrape into a right-angle joint at the neck or bridge from each side, using a small, sharp chisel. Next, remove any blemishes in the wood. Sand out light scratches and use a water-based wood filler to cover deep scratches with torn wood fibers. To remove a dent, put a drop of water in the dent, allow it to soak in, place a damp cloth over the area, and heat it with the tip of a household iron. Keep the heat away from glue joints.

57. **Sand the wood smooth.** Let us assume that during construction you sanded up through the grades to 220-grit paper. Now, eliminate any remaining scratch patterns from previous coarse papers and sand up to 400-grit. Shine a strong light across the wood to check for scratches, and sand them away before moving up to the next grade of paper. Vacuum away any traces of dust or use a tack rag (a clean cotton rag moistened with thinners and a light spray of lacquer).

58. **Select and mix the wood filler.** Open-grained woods like blackwood, koa, mahogany, and rosewood have fine pores that will appear as fine holes in the finish. You may want to apply a water-based grain filler to those woods prior to spraying on the finish. The wood filler can be mixed to match the color of the wood you're using. Make a sample board, like the one shown in the photo, to help you determine the color you want and to keep your colors uniform from one ukulele to the next.

59. **Protect the binding.** Use a cotton swab to apply thinned shellac to the binding to prevent wood filler from adhering to it.

60. **Fill the wood grain.** Dilute the filler with about 10 percent warm water until it has a creamy consistency. Apply the filler with a cloth pad and brush, working with and across the grain. Brush filler into hard-to-reach sections. Use an old credit card to scrape away excess and level the surface. Work on a diagonal across the grain. Let the wood dry and sand off the light, powdery residue with 400-grit sandpaper. Lightly wipe the surface with a moist rag to remove all traces of filler, and you are now ready to add the finish.

61

61. Spray on the finish. I recommend using a nitrocellulose lacquer finish, which gives the instrument a brighter-sounding tone than oil-based finishes and is fairly easy to apply. These lacquers are available ready for the spray gun or in aerosol cans. Mask the fingerboard and thoroughly vacuum the ukulele and surrounding work area, which should be well lit and ventilated. Put crumpled paper in the sound hole to mask the inside of the body. The first coat serves as a sealing coat. It will be absorbed by the wood and feel slightly rough. Allow it to dry for the recommended time and give it a light sanding. Use a cork sanding block on flat surfaces. Sanding back this first coat is a great opportunity to inspect and remedy any surface defects. Sunlight or strong lamplight at the right angle will show you where you may have missed a spot with the sprayer. Dust off the surface and apply the finishing coats; about three light coats should do the job. Allow the lacquer to set for a week, and then buff the ukulele with wax.

How to Sand and Spray Safely and Properly

- Nitrocellulose lacquer and thinners have a low flash point. Keep them away from open flames, electric heaters, or faulty switches, which could ignite them.

- Wear an approved respirator mask with two types of replaceable cartridges to protect yourself from fine sanding dust and lacquer vapors.

- Wash your hands regularly when sanding to avoid contaminating the wood with oils that will affect the adhesion of the lacquer coating.

- Practice your spraying technique with cheap cans of spray paint and an absorbent surface like a cardboard box, which will reveal any inconsistencies in coverage. Practice until you can lay down an even coat with no runs or overspray.

- When spraying lacquer, shine a bright lamp on the work so you can see its reflection in the wet surface. This will highlight any variation in the coating. You can spray wet on wet until you have an even finish.

- Build the finish with two or three light coats rather than one heavy coat.

- Sand in between coats with 400-grit paper. Remove the tooth from new sandpaper by rubbing two sheets together.

- Remove dust with a tack rag—a clean cloth sprayed with lacquer and moistened with thinners. After using the tack rag, check to be sure no threads are caught on the edge of the ukulele.

- Aerosol spray cans cool down as they are used, because the propellant changes from a liquid to a gas. A cold aerosol may start to spit droplets of lacquer onto the surface, ruining your work. If you spray on a cool day, use two cans and place them in warm to hot water. Use one until it begins to feel cool; return it to the water and switch to the other can.

- Dilute the first sealer coat of lacquer by 10 percent to aid absorption and sanding.

- Spraying in very humid weather may produce a milky bloom. Another coat of lacquer will remove it. You can avoid the problem by waiting for a change in the weather.

- Too much air pressure can result in a coating that looks a little like a very fine sprinkling of white dust on the lacquer surface. You can remove it with fine steel wool and furniture polish.

INSTALL THE TUNERS AND STRINGS

You can use either geared or friction peg tuners. Geared tuners give you more control over the tuning and are almost exclusively used on concert and other large ukes. If you use geared tuners, fit them so the round gear casing is closest to the body end and the shaft and knob face the head end. Friction peg tuners will need to be tightened a few times to seat them, and they may need adjustment from time to time to compensate for wood shrinkage.

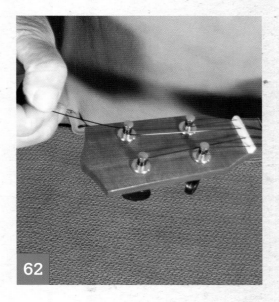

62

62. **String each tuner.** Knot a string to the bridge, pull it tight, and run it up over the nut. Wind it neatly around the tuner from the bottom, up the shaft and through the hole without any overlap. Stretch the string slightly and then tune up. You will need to retune a few times before the string and knots settle in. Repeat with the other strings.

63. **Check the strings for problems.** Strum the ukulele and check that the strings are close enough to the frets for easy playing and do not buzz. If the strings buzz on one fret, but not another, this usually indicates the fret height is uneven. Remove the strings and lightly dress the fret with a fine file or diamond lap stone. Just take a whisker off; if you have a fret crowning file, use it to round over the frets.

64. **Adjust the bridge saddle.** The bridge saddle should be adjusted so the strings are about ⅛" (3mm) above the twelfth fret. After the ukulele has been played for a while, you can fine-tune the nut slots and bridge height to suit the player. Take your time with the set up and enjoy playing your new ukulele. Solid wood stringed instruments, like the luthiers who build them, improve with age. This sometimes happens very quickly, but rest assured it will happen. Your creation will give you pleasure for many years to come.

Ukulele Bartt and the UB6

Ukulele Bartt is a rising musician on the ukulele scene, particularly in California. Backed by a band of six other musicians, known as the Ukulele Bartt Sextet (UB6), Bartt has become famous for his "Flamenculele" style of playing. Just like the word implies, this type of music involves playing the ukulele using Flamenco style. But that's not all Bartt can do—he's known for playing everything from blues to jazz to classic rock ballads. His rendition of Queen's "Bohemian Rhapsody" has become a major hit on YouTube. Bartt has also had the opportunity to work with ukulele legend Bill Tapia. You can look forward to seeing even more of Ukulele Bartt in the future as his popularity continues to grow.

CHAPTER 5

How to Set Up and Play Your Ukulele

Now that you've completed all the work to build your own ukulele, you get to enjoy using your instrument. This is the fun part—tuning your ukulele and playing a song on it for the first time.

Ukulele Tip:

Occasionally wipe down the strings of your ukulele with rubbing alcohol to remove oils and improve the tone.

WAYS TO TUNE A UKULELE

You can tune the ukulele to a piano, tuning fork, pitch pipe, or an electronic tuner. Be aware that the strings will go out of tune for a while until they settle in and the knots take up. So, with a newly built ukulele, tune it every time you play. This will also help you develop an ear for the tuning.

You have several different options for tuning your instrument, as listed above, but if you are just starting out and have no experience playing other instruments, the best approach is to buy an electronic ukulele tuner or use an online tuner. These types of tuners will tell you which string you are tuning and whether to tighten or loosen it. If you need help getting started, take your ukulele to the music store where you will be buying your tuner and ask the salespeople for help. They will love to see your new creation.

Making it all worthwhile. Strumming and singing is the payoff for all the hours spent making your first ukulele.

HOW TO PLAY A UKULELE

Examine photographs and YouTube clips of ukulele players. Study how they hold their ukuleles to find a comfortable playing position that suits you. Strum the strings a few times with your forefinger and settle into a comfortable rhythm. Now, to produce a clear clean sound you will need to learn to hold some chord shapes with your other hand.

To begin, use two chords. (A chord is a series of notes played simultaneously). On a ukulele, as on other stringed instruments, you create a chord by holding down one or more strings along the neck. Your finger effectively shortens the string, changing its pitch. A chord is named for its root note (the dominant note of the chord; also the lowest note if the chord is not inverted). For starters, you'll use the chords C major and F major.

The images at the right show the chord charts for C and F; they tell you which fingers to use on which strings. You use your ring finger to play C, for example. Chord charts are either written above or embedded in the lyrics of a song, so you know which cord to play and when to change to a different chord.

Learn these two basic chords. Get the feel of changing from one to the other, and practice until you are able to change fairly easy. When practicing, listen for the sound of each chord and train your ear to pick up the differences between the two when you switch from one to the other.

C major

F major

If you'd like some more detailed guidance on learning to play your newly built instrument, check out *Learn to Play the Ukulele*, also by Bill Plant. Even if you know how to play the ukulele, this book will open your eyes to new techniques and tips that can improve your skills. Inside you'll find:

- Exercises to help you practice
- Easy-to-read chord charts with accompanying photos
- Fun songs to play

A CD is included, containing all the exercises and songs found in the book to help you as you learn. It's a great way to develop your playing technique and style and embark on a wonderful musical experience.

YOUR FIRST SONG

The sensational "Polly Wolly Doodle" is your first song selection. You will notice a couple of things about this song: every verse and chorus starts and finishes on the F chord, and the chord changes always take place on the word "day" or a word that rhymes with "day." Each verse and chorus has the same chord pattern. The chord changes are highlighted for easy playing.

Stick with this song until you can play it really well. If you want to learn more, pick up a copy of *Learn to Play the Ukulele* and become a true master of the instrument!

Ukulele Fact:

Israel Kamakawiwo'ole primarily played a tenor ukulele made by Martin.

First verse

*Oh, **F** I went down south for to see my Sal,*
 *Singing Polly Wolly Doodle all the **C** day,*
My Sal, she is a saucy gal,
 *Singing Polly Wolly Doodle all the **F** day!*

Chorus

***F** Fare thee well, fare thee well, fare thee well my fairy **C** fey,*
 For I'm goin' to Louisiana,
For to see my Susyanna,
 *Singing Polly Wolly Doodle all the **F** day!*

Second verse

***F** Behind the barn, down on my knees,*
 *Singing Polly Wolly Doodle all the **C** day,*
I thought I heard a chicken sneeze,
 *Singing Polly Wolly Doodle all the **F** day!*

Repeat Chorus

Third verse

***F** Oh, a grasshopper sittin' on a railroad track,*
 *Singing Polly Wolly Doodle all the **C** day,*
Pickin' his teeth with a carpet tack,
 *Singing Polly Wolly Doodle all the **F** day!*

Repeat Chorus

Fourth verse

***F** I came to a river and I couldn't get across,*
 *Singing Polly Wolly Doodle all the **C** day,*
I jumped on a gator 'cause I thought it was my hoss,
 *Singing Polly Wolly Doodle all the **F** day!*

Repeat Chorus

Aloha Oe

Aloha Oe was written by Queen Lili'uokalani in the late 1800s. A copy of the song in the Queen's handwriting is kept at the Bishop Museum in Honolulu.

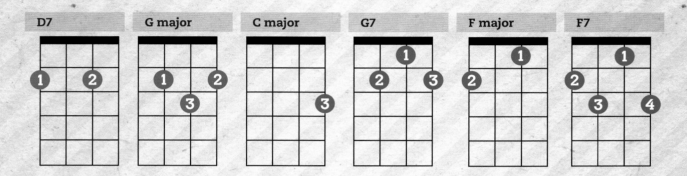

Hawaiian Version:

First verse

G Ha`aheo ka **C** ua i nâ **G** pali
 Ke **D7** nihi a`ela i ka nahele
E u-**G** hai ana pa-**C** ha i ka li-**G** ko
 Pua `â-**C** hihi lehua **D7** o u-**G** ka **G7**

Chorus

A-**C** loha `oe, a-**G** loha `oe
 E ke **D7** onaona noho i ka **G** li-**G7** po
One **C** fond embrace,
 A **G** ho`i a`e au
Un-**D7** til we meet a-**G** gain

Second verse

G `O ka hali`a alo-**C** ha i hiki **G** mai
 Ke ho-**D7** ne a`e nei i
Ku`u Manawa
 `O `o-**G** e nô ka`-**C** u ipo alo-**G** ha
A lo-**C** ko e ha-**D7** na **G** nei **G7**

Repeat Chorus

Third Verse

G Maopopo ku`u `i-**C** ke i ka na-**G** ni
 Nâ **D7** pua rose o Maunawili
I lai-**G** la hia`i-**C** a nâ ma-**G** nu
 Mi-**C** ki`ala i ka **D7** nani o ka li-**F** po **F7**

Repeat Chorus

Translation:

First verse

Proudly swept the rain by the cliffs
 As it glided through the trees
Still following ever the bud
 The `ahihi lehua of the vale

Chorus

Farewell to you, farewell to you
 The charming one who dwells in the shaded bowers
One fond embrace,
 'Ere I depart
Until we meet again

Second verse

Sweet memories come back to me
 Bringing fresh remembrances
Of the past
 Dearest one, yes, you are mine own
From you, true love shall never depart

Repeat Chorus

Third Verse

I have seen and watched your loveliness
 The sweet rose of Maunawili
And 'tis there the birds of love dwell
 And sip the honey from your lips

Repeat Chorus

What it's all about. Joining other musicians at a songfest lets you connect with them in a unique and very satisfying way.

Ukulele Fact:

James Hill and Jake Shimabukuro are two of today's most well known ukulele musicians.

Ukulele Festivals

Here is a listing of ukulele festivals worldwide, courtesy of the Ukulele Hunt website, *http://ukulelehunt.com*. Dates and times have a way of changing, and it has been known to rain. Check details before you make reservations to attend a festival.

U.S. and Canada

Hayward, California
Ukulele Festival of Northern California
Performers, food, raffle, arts and crafts.
www.ukulelefestivalnorcal.org

St. Helena, California
Wine Country 'Ukulele Festival
Concerts, workshops, jam sessions, open mic,
concert/luau, wine tasting.
http://winecountryukefest.com

Tampa Bay, Florida
The Tampa Bay Ukulele Getaway
Performances, workshops, vendors, raffle, jam sessions, luau.
www.tampabayukulele.com

Waikiki, Hawaii
Ukulele Festival Hawaii
Performers, vendors, food, ukulele orchestra of eight
hundred students.
www.ukulelefestivalhawaii.org

Waikoloa, Hawaii
Waikoloa Ukulele Festival
Performers, sing-alongs, ukulele giveaways, food.
www.ukulelefestivalhawaii.org

Kahului, Hawaii
Maui Ukulele Festival
Performers, door prizes, food.
www.ukulelefestivalhawaii.org

Needmore, Indiana
Ukulele World Congress
Lessons, jam sessions, performances, bonfire.
http://ukuleleworldcongress.wordpress.com

New Haven, Missouri
Mighty MO Riverfront Ukefest
Workshops, jam sessions, open mic, vendors,
performing artists.
www.mightymoukefest.com

Reno, Nevada
Play Uke Gatherings
Ongoing series of local concerts.
www.playuke.net

New York, New York
New York Uke Fest
Workshops, performers, jam sessions, vendors.
www.nyukefest.com

Hood River, Oregon
Gorge Uke Fest
Concerts, jam sessions.
www.gorgeukuleles.org

Dallas, Texas
Lone Star Uke Fest
Open mic, workshops, concerts
www.lonestarukefest.com

Vancouver, British Columbia
Ruby's Ukes
Ongoing series of workshops and events.
rubysukes.vpweb.ca

United Kingdom and Ireland

Cheltenham, England
Ukulele Festival of Great Britain
Performers, play-a-longs, workshops, vendors, food.
www.ukulelefestival.co.uk

Dublin, Ireland
Ukulele Hooley
Performers, workshops, jam sessions.
www.ukulelehooley.com

Europe

Sint-Niklass, Belgium
Belgian Ukulele Festival
Concerts, jam sessions, open mic.
Visit the Belgian Ukulele Festival page on Facebook.

Lerrain, France
FIUL: Festival International de Ukulele de Lerrain
Jam sessions, open mic, workshops.
http://fiul.weebly.com

Paris, France
Ukulele Boudoir
Performers, workshops, classes.
http://festival.ukuleleboudoir.com

Bocholt, Germany
The Ukulele Hotspot Winterswijk
Concerts, open mic.

Barcelona, Spain
Ukefesta
Classes, concerts, open mic, jam sessions.
http://ukefesta.com/en

Australia and New Zealand

Cairns, Australia
Cairns Ukulele Festival
Performers, world's largest ensemble, art exhibition.
http://cairnsukulelefestival.net

Melbourne, Australia
Melbourne Ukulele Festival
Performers, workshops, makers, open mic, jam sessions.
www.muf.org.au

Katikati, New Zealand
Katikati Ukulele Festival
Performers, play-along, workshops, open mic.

Asia

Thailand
Thailand Ukulele Festival
Performers, sing-along.
www.thailandukulelefestival.com

Ukulele Fact:

Paul McCartney's "Concert for George" featured songs on the ukulele in honor of George Harrison.

Information and Resources

SUPPLIES

Tonewood Supplies

Cook Woods
Twenty-five varieties of tonewood, including figured bubinga, curly and quilted maple, and jacaranda pardo.
1-877-672-5275
www.cookwoods.com

East Coast Specialised Timber
Tasmanian tonewood; figured blackwood, tiger myrtle, myrtle, black heart sassafras, and King Billy pine; celery top pine and huon pine for soundboards.
www.toptassiewoodcrafts.com.au

Hawaiian Hardwoods Direct
Figured Hawaiian koa (*Acacia koa*), figured mango (*Anacardiaceae mangifera*).
www.curlykoa.com

My Tonewoods
Mahogany (*Swietenia mahogani*), Indian rosewood (*Dalbergia latifolia*), and figured Amboyna (*Pterocarpus indicus*).
www.mytonewoods.com

West Penn Hardwoods
Wide selection of hardwoods.
716-373-6434
www.westpennhardwoods.com

Luthier Supplies

DePaule Supply
541-607-8971
www.luthiersupply.com

Stewart MacDonald
800-848-2273
www.stewmac.com

Woodworking Tools and Supplies

Highland Woodworking
800-241-6748
www.highlandwoodworking.com

Rockler Woodworking and Hardware
1-800-279-4441
www.rockler.com

Woodcraft
1-800-225-1153
www.woodcraft.com

FEATURED UKULELE MAKERS

Paul Celentano, North Carolina
http://celentanowoodworks.etsy.com

Luke Davies, Australia
www.lukerdavies.com
Contact: lrdavies2@yahoo.com.au

Jerry Hoffmann, Missouri
www.boatpaddleukuleles.com

Peter Hurney, California
www.pohakuukulele.com

Jay Lichty, North Carolina
http://lichtyguitars.com

Daniel Luiggi, Argentina
www.luiggiluthier.com
Contact: luiggiluthier@yahoo.com.ar

Chuck Moore, Hawaii
www.moorebettahukes.com

Mya-Moe Ukuleles, Washington
http://www.myamoeukuleles.com

Keith Ogata, Hawaii
http://asdhawaii.com

Palm Tree Ukuleles, Colorado
http://palmtreeukuleles.com

Bill Plant, Australia
Contact: billplant23@gmail.com

Gary Zimnicki, Michigan
www.zimnicki.com

Ukulele Tip:

Check out Jake Shimabukuro's ukulele rendition of "While My Guitar Gently Weeps," one of the most popular ukulele YouTube videos.

ASSOCIATIONS AND GUILDS

ASIA, Association of Stringed Instrument Artisans

A nonprofit trade association for instrument makers.
www.asiartisans.org

Guild of American Luthiers

A nonprofit organization that facilitates learning about the art, craft, and science of lutherie.
www.luth.org

LuthierBuilt

An international community of those involved in the craft of creating musical instruments, including makers, suppliers, and restoration experts. The organization seeks to connect these craftsmen with musicians and others around the world.
www.luthierbuilt.net

LINKS

Frets

A website with information and links about instrument making, maintenance, and repair.
www.frets.com

The Musical Instrument Makers Forum

An online community with forums for all manner of instrument makers and links to tool suppliers.
www.mimf.com

Uke Hunt

Here, you'll find a list of ukulele festivals and other great ukulele stuff.
http://ukulelehunt.com

Ukulele Boogaloo

This site includes links to organizations and clubs, performers' websites, instructional information, songbooks, and ukulele makers and retailers.
www.alligatorboogaloo.com/uke

Ukulele Underground: A Ukulele Forum

This site includes forums for beginners, contests, regional get-togethers, and more.
www.ukuleleunderground.com

Index

ACQUISITION EDITOR: *Peg Couch* ■ COPY EDITORS: *Paul Hambke and Heather Stauffer* ■ COVER/LAYOUT DESIGNER: *Jason Deller*
DEVELOPMENTAL EDITOR: *David Heim* ■ EDITOR: *Katie Weeber* ■ PROOFREADER: *Lynda Jo Runkle*

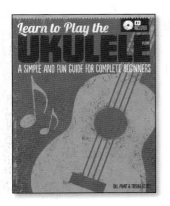

Learn to Play the Ukulele
A Simple and Fun Guide For Complete Beginners (CD Included)
By Bill Plant and Trisha Scott

With the help of this book and companion CD, anyone can learn to play the ukulele overnight.

ISBN: 978-1-56523-565-6
$17.95 • 64 Pages

Violin Making, 2nd Edition
An Illustrated Guide for the Amateur
By Bruce Ossman

Make sweet music on a hand-crafted violin. All you need are just a few common tools, wood, and the simplified violin-making process found in this newly revised and updated book.

ISBN: 978-1-56523-435-2
$19.95 • 104 Pages

Handmade Music Factory
The Ultimate Guide to Making Foot-Stompin Good Instruments
By Mike Orr

Learn how to make eight of the most unique and imaginative instruments found anywhere—from a one-string guitar made from a soup can, to a hubcap banjo.

ISBN: 978-1-56523-559-5
$22.95 • 160 Pages

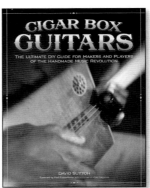

Cigar Box Guitars
The Ultimate DIY Guide for the Makers and Players of the Handmade Music Revolution
By David Sutton

Part DIY guide, part scrapbook—this book takes you behind the music to get a glimpse into the faces, places, and workshops of the cigar box revolution.

ISBN: 978-1-56523-547-2
$26.95 • 200 Pages

The Wine and Beer Maker's Year
75 Recipes for Homemade Beer and Wine Using Seasonal Ingredients
By Roy Ekins

Join the thousands of amateur wine and beer makers in this enjoyable, cost saving hobby using seasonal ingredients and recipes to create great tasting beverages.

ISBN: 978-1-56523-675-2
$12.95 • 144 Pages

The Art of Steampunk
Extraordinary Devices and Ingenious Contraptions from the Leading Artists of the Steampunk Movement
By Art Donovan

Dive into the world of Steampunk where machines are functional pieces of art and the design is only as limited as the artist's imagination.

ISBN: 978-1-56523-573-1
$19.95 • 128 Pages

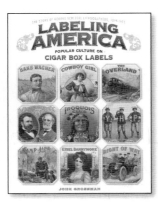

Labeling America: Popular Culture on Cigar Box Labels
The Story of George Schlegel Lithographers, 1849-1971
By John Grossman

Discover this historic collection of beautiful lithographic cigar box labels and bands from the 19th and 20th centuries, currently being housed at the Winterthur Museum in Delaware.

ISBN: 978-1-56523-545-8
$39.95 • 320 Pages

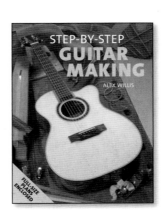

Step By Step Guitar Making
Full-Size Plans Enclosed
By Alex Willis

Making an acoustic guitar is easier than you think. Fully illustrated instructions take you through the process with ease.

ISBN: 978-1-56523-331-7
$22.95 • 144 Pages